GREAT ELIZABETHANS

HM QUEEN ELIZABETH II

& 25 AMAZING BRITONS FROM HER REIGN

Written by

Imogen Russell Williams

nosy crow

Illustrated by

Sara Mulvanny

D1332264

First published 2022 by Nosy Crow Ltd
The Crow's Nest, 14 Baden Place,
Crosby Row, London, SE1 1YW, UK

Nosy Crow Eireann Ltd
44 Orchard Grove, Kenmare,
Co Kerry, V93 FY22, Ireland

www.nosycrow.com

ISBN 978 1 83994 639 4

Nosy Crow and associated logos
are trademarks and/or registered
trademarks of Nosy Crow Ltd.

Text © Imogen Russell Williams 2022
Illustrations © Sara Mulvanny 2022

Printed in Latvia by Livonia Print

Papers used by Nosy Crow are made from
wood grown in sustainable forests.

1 3 5 7 9 8 6 4 2

MIX
Paper from
responsible sources
FSC® C002795

CONTENTS

INTRODUCTION

Over the last 70 years, thousands of extraordinary people who call Britain home have brightened and changed this country – and the world beyond it. And one of these brilliant Britons who saw it all happen was a little girl nicknamed Lilibet, who grew up to become Queen Elizabeth II.

When Queen Elizabeth was born in 1926, the world looked very different to the one we know today. Just a few months before her birth, one of the very first television sets ever made had been displayed in Britain by the inventor John Logie Baird. However, most people in the country wouldn't see or own a television until many years later. Queen Elizabeth never watched cartoons when she was little, or went on YouTube – in fact, the Internet and the World Wide Web (invented by Tim Berners-Lee, page 42) wouldn't exist until the 1980s! As a grown-up, though, she often appeared on TV herself, and her coronation was the very first one to be watched live on television by thousands of people.

When she was a child, Queen Elizabeth lived through the upheaval and destruction caused by the Second World War. The war affected thousands of other children too, like the writer Judith Kerr (page 22), who came to England because the Nazi government in Germany treated her family very badly because they were Jewish, or the actor Ian McKellen (page 32), who slept under the kitchen table when he was a little boy in case his home in Wigan was bombed.

At age 25, Queen Elizabeth came to the throne in a world that was changing quickly. The war had ended, but life after the conflict was very different for many people. Ways of living that had stayed the same for hundreds of years had been disrupted, and lots of people in Britain had now started to think differently about the world and their places in it.

Many people wanted to change things in the country for the better, like providing healthcare for everyone, not just those who could pay doctors' bills. Aneurin Bevan (page 14) founded the National Health Service (NHS), to ensure that everyone could be looked after when they become ill.

Britain was also changing in other ways. For many years, it had ruled over a group of other countries, called the British Empire. Britain had invaded these countries to control their resources and treated many people who lived in them very unfairly. Over time, people began to realise how wrong this was, and many of these countries, such as India, now started to become independent from Britain and the Empire. Eventually, a new group of countries was formed called the Commonwealth, who decided to recognise the Queen as the Head of the Commonwealth but ruled their countries completely independently of Britain.

During her reign, Queen Elizabeth visited the countries of the new Commonwealth many times. As Queen, it was her job to help the transition from Empire to independence and try to keep friendly ties between Britain and the nations it had once governed.

Many people from Commonwealth countries, like Barbados and Jamaica, came to Britain to work and to make new homes. This wasn't always easy – they were sometimes made to feel very unwelcome, even though they had been asked to come, and faced racism and abuse. In 1965, the campaigner Paul Stephenson (page 30) fought successfully to get the first law passed that said Britons of all skin colours must be treated equally. Now, the writer Malorie Blackman's (page 46) gripping *Noughts and Crosses* books show readers all over the world how racism continues to affect people's lives, both in Britain and elsewhere.

As Queen Elizabeth's reign went on, people all over the country were creating, inventing and doing amazing things. Scientists like Stephen Hawking (page 34) made discoveries that allowed us to understand the universe better. The music that people liked listening to changed over and over again, from Beatlemania in the 1960s (page 36) to rock like Queen's in the 1970s (page 40), to grime like Stormzy's in the 2010s (page 58). Activists like Malala Yousafzai (page 60) fought for women's rights around the world, so that all women can vote in government elections or have access to education. LGBT+ people campaigned for an end to hatred and discrimination, to try and make sure that people should never be ashamed or be treated cruelly because of how they feel, in the way Alan Turing (page 16) experienced.

And through the work of many talented scientists and environmentalists, we began to understand much more about the dangers of climate change caused by global warming. Like the environmentalists David Attenborough (page 24) and Chris Packham (page 44), Queen Elizabeth cares strongly about the Earth and the natural world, and understands the work we all have to do to protect the planet in the future.

During the 70 years of her reign, Queen Elizabeth has seen technology move from the very first days of television to smart computers you can carry in the palm of your hand – to do everything from buying food to talking to people all around the world! She has lived through wars, losses, fantastic sporting events like the 2012 Olympic Games and serious challenges like the COVID-19 pandemic that began in 2020. She has been Queen in a time when Britain and the rest of the world have changed, and kept on changing – and she has had to change too. But she has worked hard throughout her life to do her best for Britain and the Commonwealth, and all the amazing Britons who have helped shape the country we know today.

HM QUEEN ELIZABETH II

HM Queen Elizabeth II is the longest-reigning monarch in British history – but when she was born, nobody thought she would ever become Queen!

CAREFREE CHILDHOOD

On 21st April 1926, in a handsome house in Mayfair, London, a baby girl, Princess Elizabeth Alexandra Mary, was born to Prince Albert, Duke of York, and his wife, who was also called Elizabeth. This new princess was third in line to the throne, but no one thought she would ever grow up to be Queen. Her uncle, Edward, was going to be the next King – and if he had children, they would rule after him.

This meant that little Lilibet (as she was called) enjoyed a carefree childhood. She and her younger sister, Princess Margaret, were taught at home by a governess. They had lessons in the morning and then games, singing and dancing in the afternoons. She liked to play in her nursery with toy horses, as well as riding real ones, and she loved dogs and other animals too – especially cows!

Princess Elizabeth was one of the few people in the Royal Family who wasn't afraid of her stern, grumpy grandfather, King George V. She called him "Grandpa England", and he adored her.

But when Princess Elizabeth was 10, her uncle, who was now King Edward VIII, decided he wanted to stop being King, and her father became King George VI in his place. It was a sudden and unexpected change for the whole family. They moved into Buckingham Palace, and Princess Elizabeth immediately began to have more lessons that would prepare her to become the Queen one day, after her father. She learned about law, royal etiquette and manners, and the history of government.

HELPING IN THE WAR

When Princess Elizabeth was 13, the Second World War broke out. Like many children, she and Princess Margaret were sent away from London, because of the dangers of bombing raids. The two sisters spent the war living at Windsor Castle. However, when she finally turned 18 in 1944, she wanted to help. She trained as an ambulance driver and truck mechanic with the Auxiliary Territorial Service (ATS). Princess Elizabeth was very popular, especially when pictures of her mending trucks or behind the wheel of an ambulance appeared in the newspapers!

During the war, Princess Elizabeth had also met Prince Philip of Greece, and fallen in love with him. Although her parents were unsure about the relationship, Princess Elizabeth knew she wanted to marry him, and eventually the King allowed them to become engaged. They were married in 1947, and soon had two children – Prince Charles, born in 1948, and Princess Anne, two years later. (They would later have two more sons, Prince Andrew and Prince Edward.)

In 1952, Princess Elizabeth's father died. At the age of 25, having weathered a world war, got married and had two children, little Lilibet was now Queen Elizabeth II.

The Crown Jewels pass from monarch to monarch, but Queen Elizabeth also owns a lot of other amazing jewellery, including brooches, tiaras, necklaces and rings. The Imperial State Crown, which she wears for the State Opening of Parliament, is set with 2,868 diamonds!

SERVING THE PEOPLE OF BRITAIN

As Queen Elizabeth's reign continued, she recognised the country she ruled was changing. People's ways of life were becoming different, and she realised the monarchy needed to seem more up-to-date too. Rather than being seen as out of touch with normal people's lives, the Royal Family needed to show what they had in common with the public.

Queen Elizabeth also travelled widely, visiting the nations of the Commonwealth many times as well as representing Britain in other countries. She has visited 116 different countries during her reign – more than any other British monarch. When at home, Queen Elizabeth loves to spend time with her corgis – she has owned more than 30 of these dogs, though not all at the same time!

Queen Elizabeth faced many challenges during her time on the throne – disasters, acts of terrorism, losses in her own family – but she has always tried to do her duty, and worked hard to serve the people of Britain. Her birthdays and anniversaries have always been celebrated with big public events. Over 1,400 soldiers, 200 horses and 400 musicians have taken part in the Queen's Birthday Parade every year! In general, though, the Queen has always preferred royal life to be simple and straightforward, without unnecessary fuss – a belief that has served her well over the incredible 70 years of her reign.

TIMELINE

Since Queen Elizabeth II was born in 1926, the world has changed in so many ways. Here are just a few of the important events and incredible achievements that have happened during her life and reign.

1926
21st April
Princess Elizabeth Alexandra Mary Windsor (page 6) is born in Mayfair, London.

1936
January George V (Princess Elizabeth's grandfather) dies, and Edward VIII (her uncle) becomes King.

1948
The National Health Service (NHS) begins treating people in Britain (Aneurin Bevan, page 14). For the first time, people can be given healthcare for free without having to pay a doctor.

1947
Princess Elizabeth marries Philip Mountbatten, a former prince of Greece. They first met when they were teenagers and became officially engaged to be married when she was 21 years old. Prince Philip is given the title Duke of Edinburgh.

1952
King George VI dies. Princess Elizabeth becomes Queen Elizabeth II.

1953
Queen Elizabeth II is crowned in Westminster Abbey, London. The ceremony is shown on television for the first time.

1961
Roald Dahl's first book, *James and the Giant Peach*, is published, and becomes a bestseller (page 18).

1963
The Beatles (Paul McCartney, page 36) release their first album, *Please Please Me*. This leads to 'Beatlemania' all around the world!

1975
The rock band Queen's song "Bohemian Rhapsody" is released (Freddie Mercury, page 40). Although it is nearly six minutes long and considered very strange, it will go on to be considered one of the greatest tracks of all time!

1973
Britain joins the European Economic Community (which later becomes the European Union).

1936
December King Edward VIII gives up the throne and King George VI (Princess Elizabeth's father) takes his place. Princess Elizabeth is now next in line to be Queen.

1939
The Second World War begins. Germany invades Poland, and Great Britain and France declare war on Germany.

1947
India and Pakistan mark their independence from Britain. During Queen Elizabeth's reign, many countries which used to be governed by Britain become independent.

1945
The Second World War ends in Europe, when Germany surrenders.

1940
During the Battle of Britain, Prime Minister Winston Churchill (page 12) refuses to surrender. His inspiring speeches help the British people to stay determined to fight.

1965
The Race Relations Act makes it illegal to refuse to serve someone in Britain because of their skin colour, which happened to the campaigner Paul Stephenson in 1964 (page 30).

1966
England win the World Cup 4-2 against Germany, with a side including Bobby Charlton (page 28).

COLOUR

1967
BBC2 becomes the first channel in Britain to broadcast in colour.

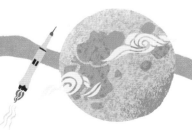

1969
The American astronauts Neil Armstrong and Buzz Aldrin land on the Moon for the first time.

1968
Judith Kerr's first book, *The Tiger Who Came to Tea*, is published (page 22).

1967
Homosexuality is legalised in the UK (for men aged 21 and over). This means people like Alan Turing (page 16) will no longer face prosecution or punishment for being gay.

1979
David Attenborough's nature documentary *Life On Earth* is broadcast for the first time (page 24).

1983
The Internet is invented – all computer networks can now speak to each other using a universal computing language.

1988
The scientist Stephen Hawking's book *A Brief History of Time* is published (page 34). It will go on to sell more than 10 million copies!

2004
At the Olympic Games in Athens, Kelly Holmes wins gold medals in the 800-metre and 1,500-metre races (page 54).

2002
Queen Elizabeth marks her Golden Jubilee year – 50 years as Queen. During this year, she travels 40,000 miles, visiting the Caribbean, New Zealand and Australia, and 70 towns and cities across the UK!

2001
Noughts and Crosses, the first book in Malorie Blackman's bestselling series, is published (page 46). *Endgame*, the last in the series, will arrive 20 years later!

2007
Apple launches the first iPhone.

2012
Queen Elizabeth marks her Diamond Jubilee year – 60 years as Queen. The singer Shirley Bassey (page 26) performs a special song at the celebrations: "Diamonds are Forever"!

2012
The Olympic Games is held in London. Mo Farah wins gold medals in the 5,000-metre and 10,000-metre races (page 56).

2022
Queen Elizabeth marks her Platinum Jubilee year – 70 years on the throne!

2021
Queen Elizabeth's husband, Prince Philip, dies at the age of 99. They had been married for 73 years.

1989
Tim Berners-Lee invents the World Wide Web (page 42). Computer users can access information via the Internet by using hyperlinks to travel between documents.

1989
Ian McKellen co-founds Stonewall, a charity that campaigns for LGBT+ rights (page 32).

1992
Tanni Grey-Thompson takes four gold medals at the Barcelona Paralympics (page 52).

2000
The 20th century and the second millennium end. The start of the 21st century and the third millennium is celebrated in lots of places around the world.

1998
The Good Friday Agreement is signed. Peace in Northern Ireland is agreed, after 30 years of conflict over whether Northern Ireland should be part of the Republic of Ireland or the United Kingdom.

1994
The Channel Tunnel, linking England and France, is opened – the Queen is one of the very first to make the journey under the Channel there and back by train!

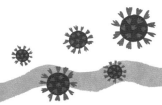

2014
The activist Malala Yousafzai becomes the youngest ever winner of the Nobel Peace Prize (page 60). She accepts it not just for herself, but "for those forgotten children who want education . . . those frightened children who want peace . . . those voiceless children who want change."

2016
The UK votes to leave the European Union (also known as 'Brexit').

2019
Stormzy becomes the first Black British solo artist to headline Glastonbury (page 58).

2020
December The Oxford AstraZeneca vaccine, designed by Sarah Gilbert and her team, is approved for use to help protect people from COVID-19 (page 48).

2020
January A new virus called COVID-19 (also known as 'coronavirus') begins to spread all over the world, causing a pandemic that makes millions of people very ill. Lots of people stay at home to help stop the virus spreading, and don't go to offices, schools or other public places for many months.

WINSTON CHURCHILL

As prime minister, Winston Churchill led Britain through the Second World War, inspiring people with his speeches and refusing to give up, however terrible things seemed.

A POWERFUL FAMILY

Winston Spencer Churchill was born in 1874 to a very powerful family. His father was a British lord and a Member of Parliament (MP) and his mother was the daughter of a wealthy American businessman. He was born in a grand house called Blenheim Palace that had belonged to his father's family for generations.

Despite his family's power and wealth, Winston's childhood wasn't especially happy. He didn't see very much of his parents, although he thought his mother was beautiful and glamorous, "like the evening star". Like most upper-class Victorian boys, he was sent away to a boarding school when he was only seven. Here, children were taught Latin and Greek, and punished harshly if they didn't do well. Winston did not enjoy learning Latin and did not get very good marks in his lessons. When he was older, he took the entrance exam for a very well known boarding school called Harrow. He only just managed to pass the exam to be allowed to go there! Although he liked this school better – he learned to become a brilliant public speaker there, despite having a stutter and a lisp – he looked back on his school days as "a sombre grey patch upon the chart of my journey".

After seeing Winston playing with his huge collection of toy soldiers, his father was determined that he should join the army. It took him three tries to get into Sandhurst, a military academy that trained officers for the British Army. However, he eventually managed it. In 1895, when he had finished his training, he joined the Royal Cavalry (a group of soldiers who ride on horseback).

Winston was known for his courage on the battlefield, and he always wanted to be where the action was. During his time in the army, he served in India and Sudan. In 1899, at the start of the Boer War – a conflict between the British Empire and two independent states in South Africa – he travelled out to the battlefield as a journalist, reporting on the war. Then, like his father, he became an MP – and he was soon well known as a powerful speaker. However, during the First World War, he was in charge of a disastrous attack on Turkey, which went so badly, with so many people dying, that he was forced to resign. Winston thought his political career was over.

SPEECHES THAT INSPIRED THE NATION

But 20 years later, just as the Second World War with Germany broke out, Winston became incredibly important to Britain. Before fighting began, he had warned the prime minister, Neville Chamberlain, that Adolf Hitler, the leader of the Nazi Party which ruled Germany, was dangerous.

After Neville Chamberlain resigned in 1940, shortly after the start of the war, Winston became prime minister. He worked closely with the American and Russian leaders to fight the Nazis. He refused to consider surrendering, even when the situation seemed desperate, and he gave speech after speech that inspired and united Britain to keep on fighting.

During the Battle of Britain, when German aircraft attacked Britain for months, trying to force Winston and the government to give up, the Royal Air Force fought them back again and again. Winston paid tribute to the courage of the British pilots: "Never in the field of human conflict was so much owed by so many to so few."

The determination shown by Winston and the British people paid off. Britain wasn't invaded. In 1945, Germany surrendered, and the Second World War was over.

Throughout his life, Winston was affected by depression, which he called "my black dog".

HERO OF THE TIME

Although Winston was voted out of power at the end of the war, he became prime minister again between 1951 and 1955, and he remained very popular. When he died, in 1965, at the age of 90, he was given a state funeral – an honour usually only given to members of the royal family.

While Winston is generally considered a hero for what he did during the Second World War, he also held some very racist views. He said that African and Indian people were inferior to white people, a belief some people criticised at the time. In 1943, when Britain still controlled India, there was a terrible famine in the Bengal region of India and up to 3 million people died. Some historians say Winston didn't do enough to help the people living there, and that his decisions actually made things worse. Although he was a remarkable and talented man, who led Britain successfully through a time of war, his inspiring actions do not mean we can't recognise his faults – and expect better today.

Winston loved animals, especially cats, pigs and dogs. During the Second World War, his poodle Rufus sneaked into a government meeting. Winston told him he hadn't asked him to join the wartime cabinet!

ANEURIN BEVAN

What do you know about the National Health Service? If you were born in Britain, you were probably born in a NHS hospital, with NHS midwives and doctors looking after you. When you have injections or visit a surgery if you're ill, that's usually part of the NHS too. Unlike in many other countries, you and your family don't have to pay to see a doctor. And this is thanks to Aneurin Bevan, the Welsh politician who set up the NHS after the end of the Second World War.

LIFE IN THE VALLEYS

Aneurin, often called Nye for short, was born in 1897 in Tredegar, a mining town in South Wales. His father was a miner and his mother was the daughter of a blacksmith. Together, they had 10 children (Nye was the sixth), but five of them didn't live long enough to grow up. There were strikes and unrest during his childhood, and poor people were often treated badly by the wealthy owners of mines and other businesses. Nye felt this injustice strongly.

Aneurin had a terrible stutter as a child, and his cruel headmaster hated him, but he was determined to overcome both of these things. He educated himself by reading books from his local library and found that he could get the better of his stutter by shouting at the top of his voice! (He became well known later on for his booming speeches.) He also recited poetry he'd learned by heart on the hills above Tredegar.

At 13, Nye left school and started work in the mine with his father and brother, but he didn't stop learning – he carried on taking out books from the library and filling his mind with new knowledge. In 1925, his father died from lung disease – something that often killed miners, who had to breathe in coal dust and harmful gases as they worked. Nye had grown up surrounded by people whose harsh lives meant they were often ill. But in Tredegar, Nye had seen something else too. Many of the miners paid a small amount of their salary – 3 pence from every pound – into a fund so that they and their families could see a doctor when they needed to. In other places, if you couldn't pay, you often couldn't see a doctor at all and many people died because they couldn't afford treatment.

FOR THE PEOPLE

In 1919, Nye won a scholarship to study in London, where he decided that socialism – a system where a country's wealth is shared equally between its people – was a better way to run a country than capitalism, where people who own businesses have a lot of wealth and power. The rich factory and mine owners might not look after their workers or pay them fairly. Nye became a trade union activist, demanding better conditions for poor people.

Soon after this, Nye was chosen as a Member of Parliament (MP) for the Labour Party, and became known for criticising other politicians whom he felt weren't on the side of working men and women. He got married to Jennie Lee, another Labour MP, in 1934. During the Second World War, which started in 1939, he often criticised the prime minister, Winston Churchill (page 12). This made him very unpopular, but he believed that many of Churchill's decisions were wrong.

Nye was proud to be a revolutionary. He described himself not as a politician but as "a projectile discharged from the Welsh valleys"!

BIRTH OF OUR NHS

After the hardship of the war, many British people wanted a change. Churchill's Conservative Party, which had been in charge of the country, was voted out and the Labour Party came to power instead. Nye was given the job of Minister of Health. He was determined to make sure everyone in Britain could have medical treatment when they needed it, just as they had in Tredegar. Although many politicians were against it – as were a lot of doctors who wanted to carry on charging people for treatment! – the National Health Service Act was passed in 1946, and the NHS began treating people in 1948. This meant that thousands of people who couldn't afford to pay could now have medical care that improved or even saved their lives.

A LEGACY FOR ALL

In Parliament, Nye was known as a prickly, difficult figure, someone who would fight to defend the rights of the underdog – not always politely. When NHS charges for dental care and glasses were introduced in 1951, Nye resigned from his job in protest. But he remained someone who was loved and trusted by the people who had elected him.

When Nye died of stomach cancer at the age of 62, the whole nation mourned. MPs wept in Parliament, and one newspaper said that there was "sorrow at every street corner" in the South Wales valleys where he came from. But his legacy – free healthcare for everyone, whether they could pay for it or not – has looked after millions of people their whole lives long, from the cradle to the grave.

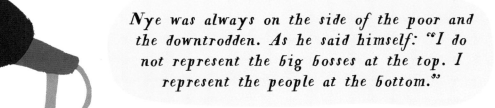

Nye was always on the side of the poor and the downtrodden. As he said himself: "I do not represent the big bosses at the top. I represent the people at the bottom."

ALAN TURING

Sometimes called "the father of computer science", Alan Turing was a brilliant thinker whose ideas helped shape the development of computers and artificial intelligence. He's also remembered for his amazing work as a code-breaker during the Second World War.

THINKING DIFFERENTLY

Alan Mathison Turing was born in London in 1912. Throughout his childhood, Alan and his older brother, John, rarely saw their parents – his father was working for the British government in India, so the boys lived with foster parents in the seaside town of Hastings.

It was clear that young Alan was a deep, unusual thinker. As a child, he was particularly inspired by a book called *Natural Wonders Every Child Should Know*, filled with descriptions of how chicks grow and why moths fly towards light. He went to school in Hastings at first, then to a boarding school in Sussex. Some of his teachers were impressed by his intelligence, but others thought he was dreamy and untidy – and things got worse when he started at Sherborne School in Dorset, aged 13.

At Sherborne, his teachers told him off for "slipshod, dirty work", and nearly stopped him taking School Certificate exams (now GCSEs). The headmaster called him "the sort of boy who is bound to be a problem for any school" – not because Alan was naughty or rebellious, but because he thought about things in a different way.

There was a general strike on Alan's first day at Sherborne School, which meant no trains were running. He was so determined to get to school on time that he cycled 63 miles!

But despite this, Alan kept his enthusiasm for science and mathematics. When he was a Sixth Form student, he met Christopher Morcom, another sixth-former who loved science. Christopher was special to Alan – they studied together and both applied to Cambridge University. Then Christopher suddenly died of tuberculosis in 1930. Alan was heartbroken, but felt that he should carry on doing the things Christopher could no longer do. So he accepted a scholarship to study mathematics at King's College, Cambridge.

Here Alan's talent was recognised at last. Aged only 22, he was made a Fellow of the college in 1935, and in 1936 he published a paper called "On Computable Numbers", which laid down the theory of how to program a computer – before computers (as we know them today) even existed.

This impressed everyone, and Alan was invited to study at Princeton University, in the United States.

CODE-BREAKER
TO NATIONAL HERO

But, across the globe, a terrible conflict was brewing – Germany, under the control of the Nazi Party, was beginning to invade nearby countries, and the world was taking sides. Alan's gift for logic meant he was brilliant at writing and cracking codes. When he returned to Britain in 1938, he was immediately asked to join the Government Code and Cypher School, the organisation in charge of code-breaking and gathering secret information. He went to live and work in their new headquarters at Bletchley Park when war broke out in 1939.

The German military used 'ciphers' to send messages, which were secret codes that their enemies couldn't read. To write messages in code, they used a cipher machine called Enigma. This machine didn't just have one simple cipher – it used wheels to keep changing the letters of the messages, making the codes almost impossible to crack unless you had an Enigma machine yourself. However, in 1941, Alan and his team were finally able to decode the messages from German submarines which had been sinking British ships as they crossed the Atlantic, when Alan invented a powerful code-breaking device called the Bombe. In 1942, he was also the first to crack the complicated codes produced by a German machine called Tunny.

Britain finally won the war in 1945, and Alan's work had played a huge part in that. He was later made an Officer of the Most Excellent Order of the British Empire (OBE). He wasn't just a genius – he was a hero.

> *Alan couldn't solve every puzzle – including the ones he set himself. In 1940, he converted his savings into silver ingots, and buried them somewhere in Bletchley Park. He returned several times with a map he had drawn, but was never able to find them!*

AN EXTRAORDINARY LIFE

After the war, Alan worked on plans for the world's first ever electronic computer, although his design wasn't the one that was finally made. He was also a pioneer in investigating artificial intelligence and developed a test (later called the Turing test) to figure out whether or not a computer was actually thinking. Then he began to look into 'morphogenesis', which is the process of how cells develop. He never stopped thinking about exciting new things to study.

His extraordinary life had a sad, undeserved ending. Alan was gay, which was illegal in Britain until 1967. When police discovered that Alan was in a relationship with a man in 1952, this was considered a crime. As a punishment, he was made to take drugs that were supposed to stop him feeling attracted to men. Two years later, Alan was found dead at his home. Although it's possible that he died accidentally, the official reason recorded was suicide. In 2009, the prime minister Gordon Brown apologised on behalf of the British government for the way in which Alan had been treated, and in 2013 the Queen granted him a royal pardon. We'll never know what other amazing inventions or discoveries he might have made.

ROALD DAHL

Have you ever dreamed of eating a Wonka Bar, moving things with your mind, or making a potion that sent your grandma through the roof? Roald Dahl's amazing stories have been thrilling children – and grown-ups! – since *James and the Giant Peach* was published in 1961.

PRANKS AND CHOCOLATE

Roald Dahl was born in Llandaff, South Wales, in 1916, but his parents, Sofie and Harald, were Norwegian. Named after the famous polar explorer Roald Amundsen, Roald would also grow up to travel far and wide, especially in his imagination. In the summer holidays, he loved visiting his grandparents in Norway, where he ate fish pudding and special many-layered cake, and listened to his mother telling stories of trolls, giants and witches.

But Roald's childhood was marked by sadness, as well as joy and adventure. When he was only four, his sister Astri died of appendicitis, and not long after, his father died too. His mother was left with six children to bring up alone.

Roald was quite a mischievous little boy. He wrote about his experiences at school in Llandaff, and later at boarding school in Repton, in his autobiography, *Boy.* One of his most outrageous pranks was when he and a group of friends put a dead mouse in a bottle of gobstoppers! When the owner of the sweet shop complained, the headmaster punished the boys so harshly that Sofie took Roald away and sent him to another school.

At boarding school in Repton, Roald hated the teachers' cruelty and having to run errands for older boys – but he loved being asked to test new chocolates for Cadbury and write down what he thought of them. This would inspire one of his most famous and best-loved books: *Charlie and the Chocolate Factory.*

FLYING THE NEST

When he left school, Roald didn't want to go to university – he wanted to find a job that would send him to some of the world's most beautiful and far-flung places. He joined the Shell Petroleum Company and went to Tanzania in East Africa.

When the Second World War broke out, in 1939, Roald joined the Royal Air Force and was taught to fly a fighter plane. Cramming himself into the tiny cockpit was very uncomfortable for him, as he was almost 2 metres tall! Roald was a gifted pilot, but one day his plane crash-landed in Egypt and he was seriously injured. He spent the rest of the war working at a desk.

Before Roald Dahl's stories, hardly anyone knew the word 'gremlin' – meaning a little mischievous creature that makes machinery go wrong. He learned it working in the RAF, and used it for his book, The Gremlins, published in 1943. Roald also invented more than 500 new words and names during his writing career!

WRITING STORIES

After the war Roald began making his living as a writer, mainly writing stories for grown-ups. In 1953, he married a film actor, Patricia Neal, and they had five children together. Through telling his children bedtime stories, Roald learned how to hold their attention and make them laugh – and he started to put these skills to use when writing his first children's books.

When *James and the Giant Peach* – the story of a little boy with two cruel aunts, a huge peach and some enormous insects – was published in 1961, it was an instant hit. After that, Roald went on to write over 20 books for children, including *Charlie and the Chocolate Factory, Fantastic Mr Fox, George's Marvellous Medicine, Matilda, The Twits, The Witches, Danny, the Champion of the World* and *The BFG*. The story of Matilda – a little girl with horrible parents, who loves reading and uses the power of her mind to move objects and fight back against cruel grown-ups – is one of Roald's best-known and best-loved tales.

Gruesome or scary things often happen in Roald's books – children may be eaten by giants, turned into mice, sucked up pipes or shrunk to a tiny size – but his tough, clever young heroes still come out on top, and young readers still love his stories! His books have sold more than 200 million copies worldwide.

Roald wasn't perfect though – he could be outspoken, and he held some prejudiced views about Jewish people that were hurtful and wrong. In 2020, his family apologised for the harm these views caused.

Roald died in 1990, when he was 74 years old, leaving behind a legacy of wonderful words and strange, exciting creations.

Roald Dahl's granddaughter Sophie Dahl is also a writer! She wrote her first book for children in 2019.

YEHUDI MENUHIN

The amazing violinist Yehudi Menuhin was born in New York, travelled the world playing with famous orchestras and settled in Great Britain, where he set up a school for other brilliant young musicians.

OBSESSED WITH THE VIOLIN

In 1916, a Russian Jewish couple, Moshe and Marutha, arrived in New York City in the United States. While looking for somewhere to live, they met a landlady who didn't like Jewish people. Not long after this, their first child was born. Defiantly, they named their little boy Yehudi, meaning 'The Jew'.

From the age of three, Yehudi was obsessed with the violin. When he heard Louis Persinger, the leader of the San Francisco Symphony Orchestra, playing, he demanded a violin of his own. But when he was given a toy tin violin for his birthday, he threw it away, complaining that it didn't sing! Shortly after that, he was given a real violin and began to have lessons with Louis Persinger himself. He was incredibly talented and learnt very quickly, playing his first public concert with Louis at the age of just seven.

When Yehudi was four, his sister Hephzibah was born. A year later, another sister, Yaltah, followed. Both sisters grew up to be talented pianists – and Hephzibah became Yehudi's favourite accompanist.

GOLD STANDARD CONCERTO

Yehudi and his two sisters were never sent to school. They studied at home with their parents – who were strict teachers and insisted on a lot of learning! After Yehudi's first concert, lots of people wanted to hear him play, and the family travelled to many different places to allow him to perform. He went to study in Paris, France, with the Romanian composer and violinist Georges Enesco. Yehudi became very fond of Georges and worked with him all his life.

In 1927, when Yehudi was 11, he played Beethoven's "Violin Concerto" at the well known Carnegie Hall in New York. All of a sudden, he was famous! After that, he toured concert halls around the world, playing music by composers like Brahms, Mozart, Bach and many others. In 1932, Yehudi, aged 16, played the English composer Edward Elgar's "Violin Concerto" – with Elgar, aged 75, conducting! This recording is still thought of as the perfect version of this concerto, against which all other performances are judged.

THE POWER OF MUSIC HEALS

During the Second World War, Yehudi played to Allied troops who were fighting against Nazi Germany. Later on, accompanied by a pianist called Benjamin Britten (who would become a famous composer too), he played to survivors of the Belsen concentration camp in Germany. Over 50,000 people – mostly Jewish people – had died there during their imprisonment by the Nazis. After the Nazis had been defeated and the war was over, Yehudi was also the first Jewish musician to visit Germany to play with the Berlin Philharmonic Orchestra. Some people criticised him for doing this, but Yehudi, who believed in the power of music to heal, felt strongly that it was the right thing to do to help bring people back together.

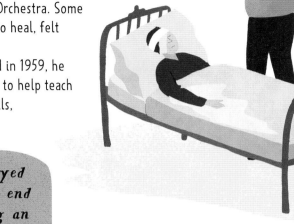

Yehudi had felt attracted to Great Britain since discovering the music of Elgar, and in 1959, he settled in London. In 1963, he set up the Yehudi Menuhin School in Surrey, England, to help teach musically gifted children with talent like his own. Here, he taught many brilliant pupils, some of whom grew up to become famous musicians too.

> *After Yehudi had played a concert, he liked to end the evening by eating an ice cream. His favourite flavour was strawberry!*

A WEALTH OF WONDERFUL RECORDINGS

Throughout his life, Yehudi was outspoken when he thought people in power were doing the wrong thing. He spoke out against 'apartheid' in South Africa, which was a set of laws that kept people of different skin colours apart and gave white people more power. He also said the bad treatment of people who criticised the Russian government was wrong. This didn't always make his life easy, but he never stopped doing it.

Yehudi loved the Western classical composers he'd grown up with, but he was also adventurous and keen to experience other types of music. He enjoyed playing jazz music, and exploring Indian music with the famous sitar player Ravi Shankar. In India, he also fell in love with yoga, which he practised daily for the rest of his life.

As he grew older, the arm he used to hold his violin bow became weaker, so he did more conducting than performing, leading many of the world's most famous orchestras. He was made first Sir Yehudi, then Lord Menuhin, but he preferred to be known just as Yehudi.

Yehudi died in 1999, leaving behind hundreds of wonderful recordings – and the joyful memories of his students and the people who had heard his extraordinary performances.

> *In 1982, Yehudi conducted Beethoven's Fifth Symphony for the Berlin Philharmonic Orchestra's 100th anniversary gala – standing on his head, and conducting with his feet!*

JUDITH KERR

If you've ever heard a *Mog* story, or read *The Tiger Who Came to Tea*, you've enjoyed the work of Judith Kerr, whose funny, gentle picture books have delighted millions of children all around the world.

A CHILDHOOD ON THE MOVE

Judith was born Anne Judith Kerr in 1923, in Berlin, Germany's elegant capital city. Her parents, Alfred, a writer, and Julia, a musician, were clever and artistic. From when she was very young, Judith loved to draw and paint. But Judith's family were forced to leave Germany when she was only nine. They were in danger – the Kerrs were Jewish, and Alfred had criticised the Nazis, a political group who hated Jewish people. When Alfred heard that the Nazis were about to take charge and he would be arrested, he fled to Switzerland, followed by Julia and the children. From Switzerland, they went to France, and eventually on to England, where they were safe at last from the invading Nazis. (Judith would later write about what it was like to have to escape to a new country in her book *When Hitler Stole Pink Rabbit.*)

Judith and her brother, Michael, learned French and English easily. However, settling into new places was harder for their parents. As refugees, the Kerrs had to live in a hotel room, relying on charity and help from friends, without a proper home of their own. It was difficult for Alfred to find work, and he and Julia missed their old life – but they had escaped the Nazis. Judith was always grateful that her family had found refuge in Britain. Although she felt like an outsider at times – she went to 10 different schools during her childhood – she still loved making quick, colourful sketches everywhere she went. She was a huge perfectionist, though – sometimes she felt like she rubbed out more lines than she drew.

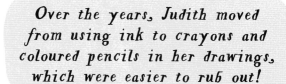

Over the years, Judith moved from using ink to crayons and coloured pencils in her drawings, which were easier to rub out!

THE TIGER ARRIVES

During the Second World War, Judith left school and volunteered with the Red Cross, sorting bandages for wounded soldiers. When the war was over, she went back to her drawing, winning a scholarship to the Central School of Arts and Crafts, and then teaching art at a school. After that, she joined the BBC as a scriptwriter and met another scriptwriter called Nigel Kneale, whom she married in 1954. When they moved into a house with a garden, Judith immediately got a cat – something she'd wanted to do for years!

When Nigel wrote his most famous show, *The Quatermass Experiment*, Judith helped him create special effects for the monster in the show by gluing leaves onto gloves!

Judith and Nigel had two children, Tacy and Matthew. Judith gave up her job to look after them, which she sometimes found boring. But Tacy and Judith loved the tigers in the zoo, which they often went to visit. To entertain Tacy at bedtime one day, Judith made up a story about a little girl, her mother and a visiting tiger who ate up all the food in the house. Five years later, when Tacy was at school, she began to turn it into a book, drawing the pictures herself. She remembered all the words easily, because Tacy had made her tell it so many times! In 1968, *The Tiger Who Came to Tea* was published for the first time and became an instant success. It has now sold more than five million copies.

There was usually a cat sitting on Judith's lap while she was working. Her ninth cat, Katinka, also featured in one of her books, *Katinka's Tail*.

THE STORY OF MOG

Judith went on to write many more books, usually based on her day-to-day family life. One was the story of *Mog the Forgetful Cat*, about a cat who forgets how to get into her house and catches a burglar by mistake – this was based on Judith's naughty tabby cat, who wouldn't use the cat flap. This book, and many other stories about Mog – including one in which Mog dies, *Goodbye Mog*, which Judith wrote to help children say goodbye to loved pets – became very popular too. Their gentle humour delighted both young children and grown-ups, and her rounded, colourful pictures were warm and cosy enough to sink into.

When Judith died in 2019, at the age of 95, she had written more than 30 books, selling over 10 million copies around the world. She was still working and talking about her books, and had just published a new one, *The Curse of the School Rabbit*. The little girl who narrowly escaped the Nazis had become one of the best-loved British children's authors of all time, bringing joy to families everywhere.

DAVID ATTENBOROUGH

Have you ever watched a nature documentary? Perhaps it was one of David Attenborough's. Born in 1926, Sir David Attenborough is a famous television broadcaster and natural historian. He is the presenter of some of the most popular and powerful shows ever made about plant and animal life on Planet Earth.

When David first started working in television, his boss thought his teeth were "too big" for him to be a presenter! He worked as a producer, camera operator, director and sound technician instead.

YOUNG EXPLORER

Although he has spent nearly all his life working as a television broadcaster, the television was only invented the year after David was born, so he didn't watch TV as a child. His father was the head of University College Leicester, and David and his brothers, Richard and John, spent their childhoods running wild and exploring the university grounds. David loved science, collecting rocks and finding badger setts and birds' nests – he even made a museum at home to display his finds.

David wasn't afraid to get his hands dirty, catching newts to sell to the university for pocket money (at 3 pence a newt – about £2 today!). He was also keen to explore and take risks – when he was 13, he jumped on his bicycle and cycled all the way to the Lake District to spend three weeks there collecting fossils. His parents had no idea where he was!

A clever and hard-working student, David won a scholarship to study Natural Sciences at Cambridge University, and joined the British Broadcasting Corporation – or the BBC, for short – in 1952.

Still fascinated by nature and wildlife, David began to present programmes like *Animal Patterns*, teaching viewers about animal camouflage and behaviour. He preferred to film animals in their natural habitats, not in a TV studio. While presenting *Zoo Quest*, David travelled far and wide to find extraordinary creatures and describe them to his audience.

A WORLD IN COLOUR

Early television programmes were broadcast in black and white. But in 1965, David was put in charge of the TV channel BBC Two, just before it began to broadcast in colour. Now that viewers could see the whole rainbow, what should be shown? He chose a range of exciting shows, from art programmes to crazy comedies, that made the channel very popular.

But although David enjoyed running BBC Two, he missed presenting and making programmes himself, especially wildlife programmes. So in 1972, he left the BBC and returned to making TV. For a long time, he had wanted to film a huge series, tracking life on our planet from its earliest beginnings to the present day. In 1979, *Life on Earth* was broadcast for the first time – and it was revolutionary.

As he looked at fossils, jellyfish and sharks, David's excitement gave his viewers a sense of getting right up close to secretive and amazing creatures. New ways of filming were used to show tiny details of animal life; camera operators would wait for hours to see a particular creature, or create fake habitats so they could film while animals slept. Viewers could watch amazing experiences, like David and a gorilla meeting face to face. The next day, the gorilla and her children groomed David as though he was one of them!

Many more award-winning documentaries followed, examining all Earth's habitats and creatures. David and his crew constantly found new ways to film the natural world – in *The Trials of Life*, medical equipment used to look inside the human body allowed them to film inside an army ants' nest!

> There are more than 20 species of plants and animals named after David, including a Caribbean bat (*Myotis attenboroughi*) and a Madagascan stump-toed frog (*Stumpffia davidattenboroughi*)!

> David wasn't the only performer in the family. His brother Richard would go on to become an Oscar-winning actor and director, starring in films like *Jurassic Park*.

SAVING THE PLANET

David is especially well known for his two recent documentaries about ocean life – the beautiful and moving *Blue Planet* and *Blue Planet II*. One episode of *Blue Planet II*, which showed a whale grieving for her baby calf killed by plastic, made viewers aware of how badly plastic pollution affects marine life. It had a huge impact, encouraging many people to start using metal straws or canvas bags to avoid filling the sea with more plastic rubbish.

Though some of his earlier programmes were more gentle or hopeful about the environment, David Attenborough is now determined to tell everyone who watches his work that we must act now to save our world. All his life, he has shown the development of life on Earth, its astonishing riches and the ways in which human activity has harmed and threatened it. Now he is using all his experience to tell us to fight back against climate change and extinction.

SHIRLEY BASSEY

Born into poverty, with many struggles to overcome, Shirley Bassey would go on to become one of the world's most successful female singers, famous for singing James Bond themes – and for the sheer power of her voice!

SCRAPING BY

In the 1930s, life in the Tiger Bay docklands in Cardiff, Wales, could be tough. The docklands were full of sailors from all around the world, determined to enjoy themselves now they were back on dry land – sometimes in a very rowdy way. But Tiger Bay was also a place where people played all kinds of music, danced and had fun together.

In 1937, a baby girl was born there, the youngest of seven children, to Eliza, who had moved there from England, and Henry Bassey, a Nigerian seaman. Things were hard for the Bassey family. There were a lot of them and they didn't have much money. Back then, it was uncommon for white and Black people to marry, so they often faced racism and prejudice. The wider world was rumbling grimly towards the Second World War. And when Shirley was only one year old, her father was sent to prison, making it even harder for her mother to support Shirley and her sisters and brother. The family moved to another place, called Splott, not far away, and scraped by on Eliza's earnings.

ALWAYS SINGING

Shirley adored her mother, who was a good cook and very pretty – and who loved to dance. She didn't like the cheap meat the family had to eat, and being cold and wearing hand-me-down clothes, but she dreamed of better things – and she sang all the time, until her sisters told her to shut up!

When Shirley was a teenager, she left school and went to work in a factory to help pay the family's bills – though she got into trouble for singing on the job! At night, she also sang in pubs and clubs to earn some extra money. She had a lot of talent and appeared in a couple of touring shows.

As well as being good at singing, Shirley was a very sporty little girl – she was good at netball, baseball and cricket.

BECOMING A STAR

Then things changed for Shirley. An agent called Michael Sullivan heard her sing and her powerful voice impressed him so much that he offered to represent her, sure that he could make her a star. He taught Shirley how to stand and move on stage, so that she could keep an audience spellbound. Then she was invited to star in a show at the Adelphi Theatre, London. After she sang on TV and impressed a record company, she was offered a recording contract – and the chance to record her own songs.

When Shirley was 19, she released her first single, "Burn My Candle", and a year later she had her first big hit with "Banana Boat Song", which reached number eight in the charts. After that, there was no stopping her. In 1959, she became the first Welsh person to have a Number One hit with "As I Love You" – followed by a second Number One three years later.

> "I knew I was a singer the first time I heard applause."

INTERNATIONAL FAME

In 1964, Shirley sang her first James Bond theme song, "Goldfinger". This made her an international star, and was followed by two more – "Diamonds Are Forever" (1971) and "Moonraker" (1979). She began to go on tours around the world. Audiences were amazed by the power of her voice and the glamour of her presence. She became known for sequinned gowns, fabulous jewellery and sheer style!

> *Shirley played the Glastonbury Festival in 2007, stealing the show in a glamorous pink dress and diamanté Wellington boots. She also sang at Queen Elizabeth II's Diamond Jubilee. What did she sing? "Diamonds Are Forever", of course!*

Shirley went on to sell nearly 140 million records over the course of her career – and she is the only person ever to have recorded more than one James Bond theme. (She would still like to record another if she got the chance!) In 1999, she was made a Dame by Queen Elizabeth II, and in 2019, she was honoured by her hometown, Cardiff, and given an award called the 'Freedom of the City'.

BOBBY CHARLTON

Bobby Charlton came from a family of fantastic footballers – but he was something extra-special, even for them! A member of the England football team that won the 1966 World Cup, he scored 49 goals for England, and is considered one of the greatest midfielders of all time.

A FOOTBALL FAMILY

On 11th October 1937, in the coal-mining town of Ashington, Northumberland, a woman called Elizabeth gave birth to a baby boy called Robert, named after his dad, Robert Charlton. Elizabeth (whom most people called Cissie) was known for her sparkling eyes and her mischievous sense of humour. Though she worked as a teacher, she loved football passionately and knew a lot about it. Her four brothers also loved football – in fact, they all played professionally. Jackie Milburn, her cousin, was a famous striker with Newcastle United too.

Cissie had wanted to be a football player herself, but back then, girls weren't able to become professional football players. Instead, she encouraged young Bobby and his brother Jack to play football, even though their dad was much more interested in boxing!

From an early age, it was clear that both boys were very talented, especially Bobby. But nobody knew that this little boy would grow up to become one of the greatest footballers ever to play for England.

Jack was outgoing and mischievous, but Bobby was so quiet and well behaved that he was nicknamed 'Little Lord Fauntleroy'!

MANCHESTER UNITED

Bobby joined Manchester United when he was only 15, still a schoolboy. Even though Cissie was so keen on football, she worried that Bobby wouldn't be able to earn a living playing 'the beautiful game' – so Bobby started an apprenticeship in electrical engineering too, just in case. But he soon signed professionally with Manchester United and never looked back.

At that time, United didn't have the amazing reputation they have now. They weren't a very successful team until manager Matt Busby hired and trained the set of incredibly talented players who would become known as the 'Busby Babes'. Bobby was one of the 'Babes', working his way up through the youth and reserve teams. He got his chance to play on the first team in 1956, scoring twice against Charlton Athletic – with a sprained ankle!

But in February 1958, a terrible tragedy happened. A plane carrying the Manchester United team, including Bobby, crashed on the runway at Munich-Riem Airport, Germany. Eight players were killed. Bobby survived, but the club struggled after the disaster, and several of the survivors never played football again.

It was hard for Bobby to recover from the accident and the sad loss of his teammates. However, a few weeks later, he managed to get back out on the pitch again – and in April 1958 he played in the England squad for the first time, scoring against Scotland.

> Over his career, Bobby Charlton scored an incredible 249 goals for Manchester United, and 49 goals for the English national team – only Wayne Rooney has scored more!

FOOTBALLER OF THE YEAR

Bobby would go on to play for England over 100 times during the course of his career. However, some of his most famous games happened during the 1966 World Cup. He scored both winning goals in England's semi-final against Portugal. And although he didn't score in the final against West Germany – which England won 4–2 – he was voted European Footballer of the Year for his brilliant playing throughout the tournament.

In 1973, aged 36, Bobby left Manchester United after 20 hugely successful years playing for the club. He became the manager of Preston North End for a while, and later returned to United to help run the club as a director.

Bobby won many awards and trophies during his career. In 1994 he was made a knight, becoming Sir Bobby Charlton, and in 2008 he was given the BBC Sports Personality of the Year Lifetime Achievement Award – which was presented to him by his brother Jack.

> As a young man, Bobby's brother Jack worked as a miner and applied to become a police officer – but the lure of football was too strong for him, and he ended up playing for Leeds United! He also played with Bobby in the England team which won the 1966 World Cup, and eventually went on to become a brilliant manager for the Republic of Ireland team. He died in 2020.

PAUL STEPHENSON

Paul Stephenson served in the Royal Air Force before becoming one of Britain's most successful and inspiring civil rights activists, campaigning for Black Britons to be treated equally in all areas of life in Britain.

DIFFERENT FROM OTHER CHILDREN

In 1937, a little boy called Paul was born in Essex in the south-east of England. His father was West African and his mother was British, of mixed heritage.

At the beginning of the Second World War, when he was three, Paul was evacuated to a care home in a village called Great Dunmow in Essex, because his mother was working in the army during the war. Paul was sometimes made to feel like the odd one out because of the colour of his skin. A teacher at his school even cut a lock of his hair to keep because it looked so different from their own. People also stared at his mother when she came to visit, because they'd never seen a Black woman in an army uniform before. But he loved playing with his friends, paddling in streams and hunting for rabbits – even if there were no other children there who looked like him.

> *Paul's grandmother, Edie Johnson, had been a successful West End theatre actress in the 1920s.*

ENGLAND WAS HIS COUNTRY

He went back to London in 1947, but even though there were more Black people in the city, he still didn't always feel welcome. He was the only Black child in his secondary school. People would sometimes call him horrible names as he walked down the street, and some teachers treated him badly at school. Paul felt strongly that he was English and that England was his country – many years later, when he wrote his autobiography, he called it *Memoirs of a Black Englishman*. But he often felt as though he didn't belong, or that other people tried to make him feel that way. Throughout his life, he would fight for the right of Black people to be fully included and valued in Britain.

> *Because Essex Council had taken good care of him as a child and fostered him during the war, Paul and his wife, Joyce, later fostered eight children alongside their own!*

THE BRISTOL BUS BOYCOTT

Paul became an Air Force cadet in 1953, and stayed in the RAF until 1960, finishing his education while he was in the service. He also spent a lot of time working with children, especially in the Scouts. This was something else he would keep on doing all his life.

In 1962, he went to Bristol in the south-west of England, to work with young people in the community. He was the city's first Black social worker. Here, he discovered that although Black and Asian people spent money riding on the buses, the Bristol Omnibus Company refused to hire them as bus drivers or conductors. Alongside the Black drivers who had been refused jobs, Paul organised a boycott of the buses, where people refused to use the buses in protest. Support for the boycott spread through Bristol and then to the rest of the country, with famous sportspeople and politicians speaking out on Paul's side. After a few months, the bus company backed down, and began employing people of colour (but Paul lost his teaching job for being "too controversial"!).

"Every generation has a duty to fight against racism, otherwise it will find its way into our country and into our homes. Addressing this challenge is our duty if we wish to seek a happy and prosperous existence."

WELL-KNOWN ACTIVIST

In 1964, Paul went into a pub called the Bay Horse in Bristol. At this time, it was still legal in the United Kingdom for pub landlords and shopkeepers to refuse to serve Black people. Paul had just bought himself a drink when the manager asked him to leave. When Paul calmly said no, the manager called the police. Paul was arrested and spent several hours in a prison cell before being put on trial. Although the policemen who arrested him – eight of them! – said that he had been violent and tried to fight them, another man who had seen everything backed him up. The judge ruled that Paul had been wrongly accused. This event helped to bring in a new law in the United Kingdom called the Race Relations Act (1965), which made it illegal to refuse to serve someone because of their skin colour.

Paul was now well known as an activist. In 1964, he was invited to go to the United States by a group of people who were trying to stop segregation (the separation of people of different skin colours) there. Paul was surprised to be stared at when he went into the hotel where he was staying. He only discovered afterwards that the hotel had never had a Black guest before.

In London, Paul worked with the famous boxer Muhammad Ali to set up a sports association for Black children in Brixton. Paul wanted them to try new activities that they hadn't been able to do before, like table tennis and pony trekking. Cheekily, Paul even managed to get Muhammad Ali to drop in on a school assembly – for free!

Paul continued to work tirelessly for racial equality and to end discrimination, and as he grew older, he was given wider recognition for his achievements. In 2009, he was given an OBE, and in 2017, he received a Pride of Britain Lifetime Achievement Award. He even has a train named after him!

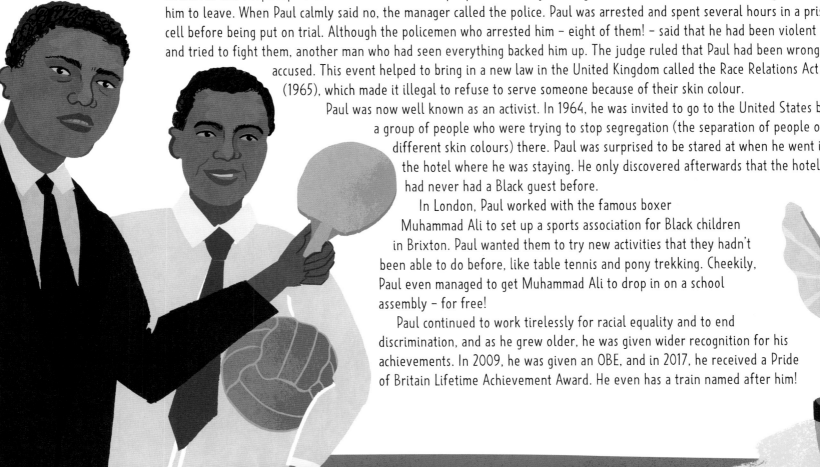

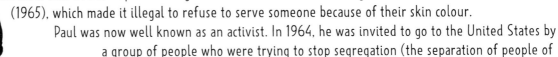

PRIDE OF BRITAIN

IAN MCKELLEN

The actor and activist Ian McKellen is best known for playing Gandalf the wizard in *The Lord of the Rings*. As well as winning awards and thrilling audiences, Ian has campaigned for the rights of LGBT+ people for many years.

A LOVE OF THEATRE

In May 1939, a few months before the Second World War broke out, Ian Murray McKellen was born in Burnley, a mill town in the north of England. His family soon moved to nearby Wigan, where Ian loved watching the traders shouting in Market Square – their playful patter showed the little boy how powerful acting performances could be, even selling apples! He also loved listening to his father, Denis, play the piano when he was in bed.

But Ian's early life wasn't always cosy – Britain was now at war, and he and his family were often afraid that bombs would fall on their home. Five-year-old Ian slept under a bomb-proof steel table, and all the windows had to be blacked out in case a glimmer of light showed an enemy plane where to target.

Despite the restrictions of wartime, Ian and his older sister, Jean, grew up loving the theatre, just like their mother, Margery. When Ian was nine, his parents gave him a folding toy theatre for Christmas, with cardboard scenery for famous plays like *Cinderella* and *Hamlet*, which could be moved with wires. At school, his English teacher often cast him in plays, especially in the miniature theatre where the boys put on shows once a term. Ian also went on school summer camps to Stratford-upon-Avon. Here, he would queue overnight for cheap tickets to see some of the greatest actors alive – even though that meant he sometimes fell asleep during the show!

At school, Ian and his friends were completely 'stage-struck', and would startle other boys by acting out scenes in the playground!

FROM STUDENT TO WIZARD

After he left school, Ian won a scholarship to study English at Cambridge University – but he acted in so many plays as a student that his scholarship was taken away! However, critics were beginning to notice his talent, and he now knew that he wanted to be an actor and nothing else. In 1961, he made his first professional appearance in a play.

Over the next 30 years, he steadily became a more successful and well-loved theatre actor, especially in Shakespearean plays. He played the lovestruck Romeo, the villainous Richard III and the powerful enchanter Prospero. And he even played a pantomime dame in *Aladdin*!

In the 1990s, Ian began to take on more film roles, and in the 2000s, he gave his best-known performances of all: Gandalf the wizard in *The Lord of the Rings*, and the metal-controlling Magneto in the *X-Men* films.

Ian has won many awards for acting, including six Olivier Awards, a Tony Award and a Golden Globe. He has also been nominated for two Oscars and four BAFTAs.

ACCEPTANCE WITHOUT EXCEPTION

But acting isn't the only thing Ian is known for. Before 1967, it was illegal for men in Britain to be gay. Even after the law was changed, another law called Section 28 was introduced in 1988, making it illegal to 'promote homosexuality' – for example, by teaching children that some families might have two mums or two dads. This law made it very hard for LGBT+ children to find support.

At that time, in an interview on the radio, Ian 'came out', and told people that he was gay himself. Because he was so well known, his honesty helped many others, although Ian did it because he felt he couldn't keep hiding: "The minute I came out, I felt immediately better in every way . . . I felt relieved that I wasn't lying." At the age of 48, he had become an activist. He went on to co-found Stonewall, a powerful charity organisation that campaigns for LGBT+ rights, whose slogan is 'Acceptance without exception.'

While he may not actually be able to do magic or control metal with his mind, Ian has used his two superpowers, acting and activism, to entertain, inspire and encourage millions of people. Thinking about his greatest achievements, he has said that his gravestone should say: "Here lies Gandalf. He came out"!

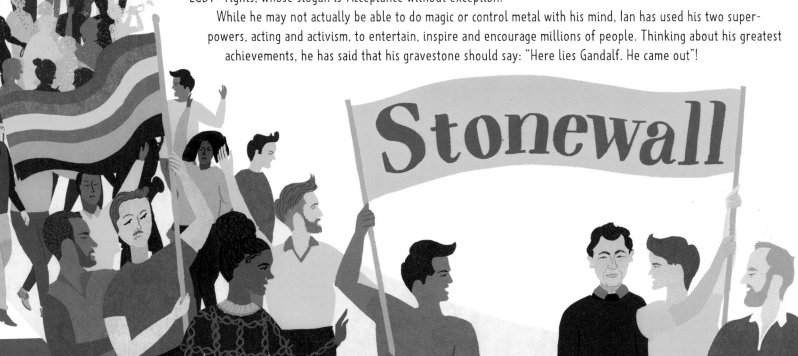

STEPHEN HAWKING

The maths and physics mastermind Stephen Hawking was told, as a young man, that a disease called ALS would hold him back and shorten his life. Instead, Stephen went on studying and asking BIG questions about the universe for more than 50 years!

BORN FOR THE STARS

In the bitter cold of a wartime Oxford winter, on 8th January 1942, a boy called Stephen William Hawking was born, exactly 300 years after the death of the great astronomer Galileo Galilei. His mother, Isobel, had gone to Oxford to have her baby because Germany had promised not to bomb the ancient city, so it was much safer there than in heavily bombed London. A few days before Stephen was born, she bought an atlas of the stars – as if she already knew her baby would grow up to study them.

Stephen's parents were intelligent and well-educated – Isobel had studied at Oxford University, and his father, Frank, was a medical researcher. They had some unusual habits, including driving around in an old taxi! Sometimes young Stephen, his parents and his sisters, Philippa and Mary, would all bring their own books to the dinner table, and everyone would eat and read in total silence.

Stephen enjoyed taking things apart – although they didn't always go back together again! As a teenager, he built a computer out of clock parts and bits of rubbish with a group of friends.

At school in London, Stephen was quickly nicknamed 'Einstein', although he didn't stand out as a student at first – he was clever, but struggled to focus on lessons and tests in class (and his handwriting was terrible!). But, encouraged by his teacher, he developed a particular interest in maths and he liked to lie outside and look at the stars.

His father thought Stephen should study medicine, so that he could earn more money, but Stephen was drawn to mathematics and physics – he hoped they would allow him to understand more about the laws of the universe. When he was 17, he won a scholarship to study physics and chemistry at Oxford University.

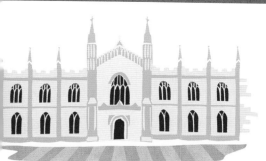

STUDYING THE UNIVERSE

After he graduated, Stephen went on to Cambridge University in 1962, where he studied cosmology – the study of how the universe first came to be and how it might end. However, the year Stephen turned 21, he had some terrible news. Doctors told him that he had a disease called ALS that would gradually take away his ability to move and speak. Many people who got ALS didn't live for very long. Stephen was told he might only have another two years left to live. He felt miserable and depressed. What was the point in continuing his studies?

But Stephen proved the doctors wrong. In 1962, he met Jane Wilde, another student, and fell in love with her. He realised that if he and Jane wanted to get married, he would need to finish studying and get a job – so he did. His brilliance meant he was quickly given a research post at a college, and he would continue to work mostly in Cambridge, studying, teaching, and coming up with new ideas, for the rest of his long life. As he became less mobile, he began to use an electric wheelchair – but he was rather a wild driver! He liked to dance in his chair at parties – and once even crashed and broke his hip while moving at speed.

From 1979 to 2009, Stephen was the Lucasian Professor of Mathematics at Cambridge – an important post held by many famous scientists in the past, like Isaac Newton.

ALWAYS QUESTIONS TO ASK

Stephen was particularly interested in the study of black holes, mysterious parts of space where the force of gravity is so strong that nothing can escape from them, not even light. His theories about them – including the idea that they gave off radiation (which would later be called 'Hawking radiation') – helped scientists understand more about these strange objects. He also developed ideas about how the world began and searched for a theory that would explain everything in the universe – though he eventually decided humans could never develop this theory, because they couldn't see all of reality clearly enough. To him, this was a good thing – it meant that there would always be questions to ask.

In 1985 Stephen caught pneumonia on a trip to CERN (the European Centre for Nuclear Research) in Switzerland. The infection nearly killed him, and it left him unable to talk. After that, Stephen spoke with the help of a computer that he worked with a muscle in his cheek.

Stephen wanted his work to be read and understood by everyone, not just scientists. In 1988, his book *A Brief History of Time: From the Big Bang to Black Holes* was published. It has now sold more than 10 million copies!

By the time Stephen died in 2018, at the age of 76 – an incredible 55 years after he was first diagnosed with ALS – he had been awarded a huge number of prizes and medals. He had helped us learn more about the universe we live in and the kinds of questions science can ask – and answer.

In his autobiography My Brief History, Stephen said of his life: "It has been a glorious time to be alive. I'm happy if I have added something to our understanding of the universe."

PAUL McCARTNEY

When the teenage Paul McCartney met a boy called John Lennon, neither of them dreamed that the music they'd make together would become famous all around the globe. With George Harrison and Ringo Starr, Paul and John became the Fab Four – also known as the Beatles!

ROCK'N'ROLL BABY

James Paul McCartney was born in Liverpool in 1942. His father, Jim, wasn't impressed at first – the new baby was all red-faced and made horrible squawking noises! Little did his dad know that this noisy baby would grow up to be one of the most famous musicians in the world.

Paul's father was also a musician, although he now worked as a salesman – he'd played jazz piano with a local band, and he loved show tunes, which inspired Paul later too. Paul's mother, Mary, who was a midwife, died when Paul was only 14. He and his younger brother, Mike, depended on their dad, who supported his sons and encouraged them to work hard for what they wanted. Music – playing it and listening to it – also helped Paul deal with his grief. He liked American rock'n'roll artists like Little Richard and Buddy Holly.

Keen to help, Jim gave the teenage Paul a trumpet for his birthday – but he soon swapped it for a guitar, so he could sing and play at the same time! On the old piano in the front room, Paul learned to thump out songs – he never had music lessons, but he had a good ear and an instinct for finding the right notes. And he was a born performer.

When Paul thought about what he might do for a living, his father advised him to become a teacher – but at that point, Paul really wanted to be a long-distance truck driver!

MAKING THE BEATLES

When Paul was 15, he met a boy called John Lennon at a church festival, playing in a band called The Quarrymen, and impressed him with his skill on the guitar. Eventually, John asked Paul to join the band. They played a combination of rock'n'roll and a kind of music called 'skiffle', which was a mix of jazz, folk and blues. George Harrison, a younger friend of Paul's, also joined, in 1958. After this, they changed their name a few times before coming up with The Beatles. They began to play more and more shows, at clubs in Liverpool and then in Hamburg, Germany. When their drummer left, in 1962, they replaced him with Ringo Starr and the legendary line-up was finally complete!

When he first heard them play "She Loves You", Paul's father suggested John and Paul should change the lyrics from "Yeah, Yeah, Yeah" to "Yes, Yes, Yes"! They didn't take his advice . . .

HIT AFTER HIT

WE LOVE THE BEATLES

The band released their first album, *Please Please Me*, in 1963. After that, 'Beatlemania' began to take over the world, as the band racked up hit after hit, from "Love Me Do" and "I Want to Hold Your Hand" to "A Hard Day's Night". Their singles and albums soon sold thousands of copies worldwide. When The Beatles appeared, in their trademark 'moptop' matching haircuts and sharp suits, their fans shrieked and mobbed them! As the band developed musically, they changed their look and sound, making albums with different influences, like *Rubber Soul*, *Revolver*, *Sgt. Pepper's Lonely Hearts Club Band* and *Magical Mystery Tour*.

Even today, The Beatles are the bestselling musical act of all time.

THE MUSIC NEVER STOPPED

But by the time The Beatles released *The Beatles* (also known as *The White Album*) in 1968, there were tensions in the band – all of its members wanted different things. After one last show in 1969, the group broke up, and its members began to make music on their own.

Paul formed a group called Wings with his wife, Linda, releasing albums like *Band on the Run* and *Wings at the Speed of Sound*, which were hugely successful.

The Beatles never reunited. Ten years later, in 1980, John was tragically shot and killed, and George died of cancer in 2001. Paul's wife also died of cancer in 1998. But Paul never stopped making music, playing concerts or experimenting with sound. In fact, he released a new album in 2020, at the age of 78!

Over the whole of his career, Paul has sold 100 million copies of his singles!

ANITA RODDICK

Born into a hardworking Italian family, Anita Roddick took one tiny little shop in Brighton and turned it into the huge The Body Shop chain, sticking to her strong environmental values all the way! She changed the way many people thought about what they bought and how they did business.

A DRAMATIC ARRIVAL

In 1942, in the middle of the Second World War, Anita Perilli was born in a strange place – a bomb shelter in Littlehampton, Sussex! She was the third of four children in her Italian family – there were very few immigrant families where she lived, which made her even more unusual. But Anita's life would more than live up to her extraordinary beginnings.

Anita's mother, Gilda, ran the family café – careful and resourceful, she recycled as much as she could, and taught her children to do the same. Anita worked there from a young age, carrying trays and running the coffee machine, and learning a lot about hard work and running a business. She often had to get up before dawn to make breakfast for local fishermen! Despite the early hours and tiring work, Anita always looked up to her bold, brave mother: "Everything I am I can lay at the feet of Gilda, the woman who went hot-air-ballooning in her eighties."

When she left school, Anita first wanted to become an actor and then she trained as a teacher, but found that wasn't her passion. Instead, she worked in France and Switzerland, and then went travelling all around the world. She journeyed through Australia, Africa and Asia, learning about how people lived in other countries and also about the products they used to care for their bodies.

When she came home to England, she fell in love with a man called Gordon Roddick, who was just as adventurous and wild as she was herself. She got married to him in 1970, and they began running a small restaurant together. Six years later, when they had two daughters, Gordon set off on a journey he'd wanted to make all his life – a horseback ride from Buenos Aires in Argentina, all the way to New York City in the USA! Anita thought this crazy idea was brilliant. She sent him off cheerfully, knowing she wouldn't see him for another two years.

THE BODY SHOP

But while Gordon was away, Anita needed to earn money for herself and her daughters – so, with a £4,000 loan from the bank, she opened the first The Body Shop in Brighton in 1976. Wedged between two funeral homes, it wasn't the best place for a shop selling beauty products! The walls were so damp that she painted them dark green to disguise the mould – the colour that later became The Body Shop's hallmark – but she made sure that it was welcoming to customers, and smelled lovely.

It was important to Anita that her soaps and lotions were environmentally friendly in every way possible. At the time, almost everyone making products like Anita's tested them on animals to be sure they were safe for humans to use. Anita utterly refused to use animal testing, which was a revolutionary decision. She also insisted that the people who supplied ingredients for the products must be paid fairly, and she asked her customers to bring containers back to be refilled – partly to save resources, and partly because they were short of bottles!

> Anita never allowed anyone to tell her she couldn't make a difference. As she said herself: "If you think you're too small to have an impact, try going to bed with a mosquito."

PRINCIPLES BEFORE PROFITS

The long hours in her mother's café had prepared her for the hard work of running a shop. The Body Shop was such a success that Anita soon opened another. When Gordon came home, he suggested letting other people open branches of The Body Shop in other places – something called 'franchising' – and the business took off.

Anita never wanted to be a huge business success – not if that meant mistreating the environment, or her workers, suppliers or customers. She certainly didn't expect her shop to become a chain that would be known and loved around the world. But by 1990, Anita was the fourth-richest woman in Britain. In 2003, when she stepped down from running The Body Shop, it had almost 2,000 stores worldwide, selling beauty products to over 77 million customers.

When Anita died in 2007, she was remembered as an activist who gave huge sums of money to counter global warming and to fight injustice, and also as a brilliant businesswoman who always put principles before profits. She changed the way millions of people thought about what they bought.

> As well as The Body Shop, Anita helped set up The Big Issue, the magazine sold by homeless people, and founded Children on the Edge, a charity that helps children affected by war and disability. Her own foundation also gave away millions of pounds to organisations like Greenpeace and Women's Aid.

FREDDIE MERCURY

A shy boy who loved music and stamp collecting, Farrokh Bulsara grew up to become the unforgettable performer Freddie Mercury, lead singer of Queen, whose amazing songs would live on long after his death.

FROM FARROKH TO FREDDIE

Farrokh Bulsara was born in 1946, in Zanzibar, which is a part of East Africa now called Tanzania. His parents, Bomi and Jer, were Parsis – people of Persian heritage, who follow a religion called Zoroastrianism. Farrokh was brought up in the same faith, which stayed important to him all his life. The family moved to India not long after Farrokh was born, and he and his sister, Kashmira, grew up there, near the huge city of Bombay (now called Mumbai).

Farrokh started learning to play the piano at the age of seven. He fell in love with making music early on – one of his school friends said later that he could play any song he heard straight away! When he was a bit older, he started using the name Freddie – and at the age of 12, he formed his very first band, which played covers of classic rock and roll songs. Calling themselves The Hectics, they wore skinny string ties and styled their hair in big 'puffs'. Freddie also collected stamps, a hobby he shared with his dad.

Freddie's voice was amazingly powerful – and the range of notes he could sing spanned four whole octaves. Most people have a range of two! Freddie believed this was because he had four extra teeth in his mouth – something which made him self-conscious about his smile all his life.

In 1963, when Freddie was 17, the family moved back to Zanzibar. But when a revolution swept the country, they had to flee, this time to England. The Bulsaras moved to Middlesex, where Freddie studied art and graphic design. He didn't forget his love of music, though. He soon joined up with a local band called Ibex, and then one called Sour Milk Sea, with whom he started singing some of his own songs. He eventually had to move out of his parents' house because the neighbours complained about the noise!

QUEEN TAKES TO THE STAGE

Then Freddie met two people who would help him create truly world-changing music: a guitar player called Brian May and a drummer called Roger Taylor, both members of a band named Smile. When the lead singer of Smile left in 1970, Freddie, aged 24, took over from him – and got the band to change their name to Queen. At about the same time, he changed his own surname from Bulsara to Mercury. The next year, the band was joined by the bassist John Deacon, and Queen's line-up was complete.

Queen's first album, just called *Queen*, and their second, *Queen II*, didn't sell many copies, but the band still carried on making music, and went on to become incredibly successful. Ten years after Freddie joined the band, tens of thousands of fans were packing stadiums to see them perform, desperate to hear songs like: "We Will Rock You", "We Are The Champions", "Another One Bites the Dust", "I Want to Break Free" and "Bohemian Rhapsody".

Freddie loved cats – so much so that he kept 10 of them, giving them names like Goliath, Tiffany and Romeo. Every cat got a Christmas stocking, filled with treats and toys – and in 1985 Freddie even dedicated an album to one of them!

UNFORGETTABLE PERFORMER

Freddie's extraordinary voice, flamboyant performing style and outrageous stage personality combined with Brian May's amazing guitar skills to wow their audiences. Freddie wore outfits like angel wings, silver-sequinned leotards, harlequin suits and royal robes during shows. Although he was shy in daily life, he moved about the stage with incredible flair, delighting the crowds with his performances.

Although he never talked publicly about it, Freddie had relationships with both men and women. During the 1980s, many people, especially gay men, died of an illness called AIDS. Freddie announced that he had the disease in 1991. He died the next day, at the tragically young age of 45 – but leaving behind a musical legacy that would never be forgotten. His assistant said he had just one regret: "that he still had music in him".

Queen's most famous song, "Bohemian Rhapsody", is nearly six minutes long! The band was told it could never be a hit when they wanted to release it, but it became their most popular track. It is often voted the greatest song ever made!

TIM BERNERS-LEE

The computer scientist Tim Berners-Lee invented the World Wide Web and was instrumental in the development of the Internet, which would completely change the way people communicate, buy things, work and learn forever.

FAMILY OF MATHEMATICIANS

In the early 1950s, two mathematicians, Mary Lee Woods and Conway Berners-Lee, met and fell in love. They had a lot in common – in fact, they were both working on a computer called the Ferranti Mark 1, which was one of the first computers that people could buy!

In 1955, their first child was born in Richmond, London – a son called Timothy, who inherited his parents' mathematical gifts. As a little boy, Tim liked model railways and trainspotting. He was thoughtful and quiet and liked working things out. His parents encouraged him to use maths to solve problems, even at the dinner table! They also talked to him about computers and what these machines could 'understand' – and the potential they had to change people's lives.

PHYSICS AND TIDDLYWINKS

Tim's youngest brother, Mike, is an impressive scientist too – he's an expert on greenhouse gases!

Tim decided to study physics at Oxford University and was very good at it. He achieved a first-class degree, but he also got into trouble for hacking the university computer with a friend. As a punishment, he was banned from using it – so he built his own computer with a soldering iron and an old television! He also found the time to play tiddlywinks against Cambridge University.

PROGRAMMING GENIUS

After leaving university, Tim worked as a programmer for a company which made traffic lights. Then, for a while, he worked on software for CERN, the huge European physics laboratory. While he was there, Tim invented a program called ENQUIRE, which stored information in 'links' that allowed a user to move easily between files. This became known as 'hypertext'.

After that, Tim designed many different computer systems before he went back to CERN, this time to work on their computer network. In 1989, he made a plan to create a hypertext system that would join with the Internet – which connected computers around the world – to allow scientists to see each other's files and results without emailing all the time. It was this plan that would become the World Wide Web, uniting the scrappy beginnings of the Internet into a huge international network.

> "The Web does not just connect machines, it connects people."

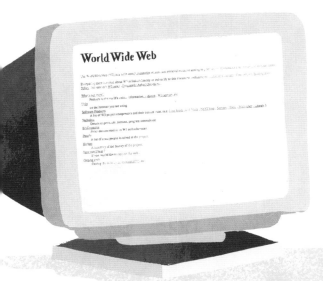

THE WORLD WIDE WEB

When Tim was given permission to develop his idea, he went on to design and build the first web browser and editor. The first site on the World Wide Web went live on 6th August 1991. It explained what the Web was and how to set up a server.

Tim didn't realise then how important his invention would be, or how the Web's popularity would explode, changing the way people worked and learned and talked to each other. Without his work, we might have no Google, no Wikipedia, no YouTube – and the Internet might belong to just a few people with the special skills to use it or enough money to buy access to it. One of the most important things about the World Wide Web was that Tim made it available to everyone, without needing to pay or sign up to anything. He believes that the Web should remain open to all, and that everyone should be able to edit it and work within it. He also believes that scientists who work with computers have a duty to keep the Web a safe place for its users.

QUIET ACHIEVER

Tim has been honoured in many ways for his world-changing achievement. He is now Sir Tim Berners-Lee and holds positions at many universities. Time magazine named him one of the 100 Most Important People of the 20th century, and he was the first winner of Finland's Millennium Technology Prize. Despite his fame, Tim doesn't live like a celebrity. When he isn't writing code or meeting world leaders, he likes to spend time quietly with his family.

> Tim was part of the London Olympics opening ceremony in 2012. As the invention of the World Wide Web was acted out, he tweeted: "This is for everyone".

CHRIS PACKHAM

The TV presenter Chris Packham is a much-loved wildlife expert, author and campaigner, who has educated both adults and children about animals and the importance of conservation for the whole of his career.

LOVING THE NATURAL WORLD

Chris was born in Southampton in 1961. From the moment he could crawl, it was clear Chris loved wild creatures and the natural world more than anything. He kept ladybirds and beetles in jam jars in his room, and studied the dinosaur pages of encyclopaedias. He loved tropical fish and reptiles and spent hours in the local pet shop, staring into cages and tanks. He thought all the time about the ways that animals lived, behaved and died.

When he was 14, Chris found a wild kestrel chick. He called it Kem and cared for it as it grew up, letting it out every day. When it became ill and died, he was heartbroken. He still remembers the kestrel, and remains fascinated by birds of prey.

As a little boy, Chris desperately wanted a bat – so much so that he called his pet mouse Batty!

SEEING THE WORLD IN DETAIL

Chris has Asperger syndrome, a form of autism, which means that he sees, hears and feels the world differently to some other people. At secondary school, he was badly bullied when he said things straight out, exactly as he saw them. But Chris sees his Asperger syndrome as a good thing – it allows him to see the world in incredible detail and sharpness. He believes it is an important part of who he is.

One of his teachers taught Chris how to preserve and stuff dead animals – a skill called taxidermy.

WILDLIFE WATCH

Chris learned all about kestrels, shrews and badgers as a teenager, and carried on doing so at Southampton University, where he studied zoology – the science of animals and how they live. As well as studying creatures, Chris was a punk rocker, playing in a band called The Titanic Survivors. To Chris, the creative, rule-breaking punk spirit went hand in hand with fighting for human and animal rights.

After he finished studying, Chris wanted to do something more creative, so he began taking photos of wildlife. He took a job as a wildlife cameraman to help pay for the equipment he needed. Soon, though, he was in front of the camera himself, presenting programmes like *The Really Wild Show* on CBBC from 1986 to 1995, which taught children about wildlife in different countries, and *The Great British Birdwatch*. With his own company, Head over Heels, Chris also made shows for the Discovery Channel and National Geographic.

Then, in 2009, he began presenting *Springwatch*, a hugely popular BBC programme which shows the movement and change of wildlife in the spring, as young creatures are born. He also presents the shows *Autumnwatch* and *Winterwatch*.

Chris has travelled all around the world, visiting places from the Everest mountain range to deserts and rainforests, as well as diving deep into the ocean. He's presented shows like *Nature's Weirdest Events* and *World's Sneakiest Animals*, giving his viewers a glimpse into the strangest and most fascinating corners of the animal kingdom – as well as filming things closer to home, like *Cats v. Dogs*!

Since the 1990s, Chris has suffered from Ménière's disease, which affects the inner ear and can make people feel dizzy, as well as affecting their hearing. He has also suffered from depression, especially after losing his dog Fish.

ACTION AGAINST ANIMAL CRUELTY

Chris believes strongly in taking action to stop the abuse of animals and to educate people about it. In 2014, he used his own money to take a film crew to Malta, where they shot footage of migrating and endangered birds being killed in huge numbers by hunters. While filming there, Chris was arrested and held for three hours – but after he was released, his footage helped raise thousands of euros for charities trying to end the hunting of birds.

Chris now lives in the New Forest, still writing, campaigning and presenting nature shows, sometimes even alongside his step-daughter, Megan McCubbin! Although there are enormous challenges facing animal lovers and conservationists today, he believes that we can rise up to meet and overcome them, and that we owe it to the world to do so.

MALORIE BLACKMAN

Malorie Blackman grew up reading and writing all the time – but she didn't dream that she would one day write books to inspire thousands of children and teenagers herself! Loved by readers of all ages, her books include the best-selling *Noughts and Crosses* series.

● BARBADOS

LONDO

A NEW LONDON LIFE

Malorie Blackman's parents arrived in England in 1960 from Barbados in the Caribbean, hoping to make a new life for their family in Britain. Malorie was born in Surrey two years later, but she grew up mostly in Clapham, a part of London. When she was three, her mother had twin baby boys – Malorie loved helping to look after her brothers, though they were a lot of work! Not long after, her two older siblings, who had been living with relatives in Barbados, came to join them in England, and the whole family was complete.

Malorie loved books and reading as a child, especially myths and legends – one of her favourite books was *The Silver Chair* by C.S. Lewis, set in the magic land of Narnia, and filled with giants, strange underground creatures, a terrifying serpent, and a prince under a spell. She read it at least 10 times! By the age of 11, she'd read all the children's books in the library, a bit like Roald Dahl's Matilda (page 18). She also wrote stories and poems non-stop herself, but she didn't dream that she might become a published writer – partly because she was Black, and all the writers she knew of didn't look like she did.

Sometimes Malorie experienced racism directed towards her – like the ticket inspector who accused her of having stolen her first class ticket when she was a teenager, or the history teacher who told her that there had never been Black inventors, scientists or pioneers. They made her feel angry and sad – and determined to make a difference.

Stormzy (page 58) namechecks Malorie in his song "Superheroes"! The grime star has said how much he loved Noughts and Crosses when he was growing up – he even has a role in the TV adaptation.

NOT SO STUPID

Malorie had always wanted to become an English teacher, but she actually studied computing at college after the school careers adviser told her she shouldn't try to train as a teacher. She worked as a computer programmer for several years, but then she was drawn like a magnet back to the world of books and stories. She wrote her first book, *Not So Stupid!*, a collection of science fiction and horror stories for teenagers, when she was 28.

Though *Not So Stupid!* was turned down by publishers more than 80 times, it was eventually published in 1990. After that, there was no stopping Malorie! She went on to write more than 60 books, including *Pig Heart Boy*, about a boy who needs a heart transplant, *Hacker*, a mystery thriller, and *Cloud Busting*, a book told in different kinds of poetry. She also wrote stage plays and scripts for TV shows like *Byker Grove* and *Doctor Who*.

Malorie was the eighth Children's Laureate, between 2013 and 2015. As Laureate, she talked about how important it was for teenagers to read for pleasure, saying that they should read what they enjoy before being forced to dive into "the classics".

NOUGHTS AND CROSSES

In 2001, her most famous book, *Noughts and Crosses*, was published. Set in a world where Black people have been "history's lucky ones", rather than white people, it imagines what would happen in a world where Black people ('Crosses') are more powerful and rich than white ones ('Noughts'), and if a Nought boy and a Cross girl were to fall in love. Malorie wrote six more books in the series – and *Noughts and Crosses* is now one of the most-read books for teenagers in the country. Malorie's books for all ages, from toddlers to teens, have inspired and delighted countless readers – and proved to many kids that brilliant writers are not just white.

Malorie has lots of hobbies. She plays the piano, drums, learns languages, composes music and loves to play World of Warcraft.

SARAH GILBERT

When an infectious disease called COVID-19 spread around the world in 2020, scientists everywhere began working to find treatments – and vaccines. Professor Sarah Gilbert was one of the first people to develop a vaccine that protected people against catching the COVID-19 virus.

FULL OF DETERMINATION

Sarah was born in 1962, in the town of Kettering, where many people made shoes and boots. Her father worked in a shoemaker's office, and her mother was an English teacher who loved opera. Sarah was a quiet girl, but clever and full of determination. When she wanted something, she worked hard to get it.

When Sarah was at secondary school, she realised that she wanted to study science, especially medicines, and worked long hours to get good results in her exams. Like her mother, Sarah also loved music – she played the oboe in the school orchestra.

> When Sarah went to study biology at university, she took up playing the saxophone – but she practised outside in the woods in case she disturbed the other students!

After her biology degree, Sarah went to the University of Hull to study genetics (how different characteristics get passed down from parent to child) and biochemistry. Then she worked for a while at a company that made medicines, before returning to university to study a disease called malaria.

In 1998, Sarah became busier still – she and her partner, Rob, had triplets! To allow Sarah to focus on her work, Rob looked after the children most of the time. Although Sarah encouraged her children to find their own interests as they grew up, all three triplets grew up to study biochemistry, just like her!

SPECIALISING IN VACCINES

After studying malaria, Sarah became a vaccinologist – a scientist who specialises in vaccines. A vaccine is a type of medicine that is usually injected into a person's body while they are healthy. It teaches a person's body how to fight off a particular virus that could cause a disease, so that if they do get infected with this virus, the body has already learned how to protect itself.

Sarah became a professor at the Jenner Institute at Oxford University. For a long time, she worked to find a vaccine that would protect against all kinds of flu virus, and to develop a vaccine for MERS (a rare illness that affects the lungs). In 2014, there was a big, deadly outbreak of a serious disease called Ebola in West Africa, and Sarah worked on a vaccine for the Ebola virus too.

But Sarah and other vaccinologists felt that the response to the Ebola outbreak had been too slow. Too many people had been infected who should have been protected. It was important to have a plan for the next serious virus that might start spreading around the world. So, in 2018, Sarah and her team began to plan for 'Disease X' – whatever that next virus might be. They took a cold virus that affected chimpanzees, and they prepared it so that it could be quickly adapted into a vaccine against any new infectious disease.

> *"The scientific process means failing quite a lot. You have to get things wrong and learn from them."*

NO ONE IS SAFE UNTIL WE ARE ALL SAFE

On 1st January 2020, Sarah read about a new kind of pneumonia that was spreading fast in a city called Wuhan in China, and realised that this might be "Disease X". It wasn't long before this new virus got given a name – COVID-19 – and started to spread further around the world, causing a pandemic. In countries everywhere, governments started making plans to help stop the spread of this serious new disease and to find treatments and medicines for it.

Thanks to their planning, Sarah and her team were prepared to rush straight into action. Once they had more information about the COVID-19 virus, they designed a vaccine within a few days!

After it was designed, the vaccine against COVID-19 was tested on volunteers for several months to make sure it was safe (all three of Sarah's triplets took part in early trials). Then it was ready to be given to the public, both in the UK and around the world. The vaccine was easy to store and transport too.

Sarah's team worked with the company AstraZeneca, who could make their vaccine. It was really important to Sarah and her colleague Catherine Green that the vaccine would be affordable for every country around the world. Sarah says that "No one is safe until we are all safe." Everyone needs access to vaccines, no matter where they live or how much money they have.

More than a billion doses of the AstraZeneca Oxford vaccine have now been given worldwide, helping to protect people – and to give them back some of the freedoms that the COVID-19 pandemic took away. In June 2021, Sarah was made a Dame by the Queen.

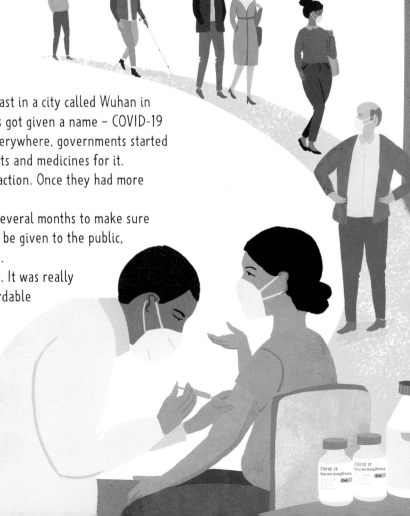

LEMN SISSAY

Though Lemn Sissay's childhood was hard and miserable, and he was let down by the people who should have cared for him, he grew up to become a brilliant writer – a poet whose work has touched and inspired thousands of readers.

FROM PLACE TO PLACE

When Lemn Sissay's mother came to Britain from Ethiopia in 1966, she didn't yet know she was going to have a baby. After her son was born in 1967, near Wigan in the north of England, she found it hard to look after him, so she asked if he could be cared for by foster parents for a little while. But instead of giving her the help she asked for, a social worker took away her baby, renamed him Norman (the social worker's own name) and gave him to a white family to adopt as their own. His mother wrote letter after letter, asking for her son to be returned, but she got no answer.

When Lemn – who didn't know his real name – was 12, his foster family decided they no longer wanted him and sent him to a children's home. They would never see him again. In homes and foster families over the next six years, Lemn was punched and kicked and racially abused, nicknamed 'Chalky White', and treated with carelessness and cruelty. As the only Black boy in most of the places where he lived, he stood out. People spat on him when he rode the bus and called him horrible names. When he painted a small part of one home's roof with the Ethiopian flag, he was sent to a secure centre where many of the children had been charged with serious crimes. Here, he was locked in a padded cell, searched and beaten. All his life, he was told that his mother had abandoned him.

> "I think I'll paint roads on my front room walls to convince myself that I'm going places."

IMAGINATION IS KEY

Lemn's sad, painful early life hurt him in many ways, but it did not destroy him. He wrote poetry to help himself express his sadness and anger, and to explore much further than his cramped surroundings. He sold his first small collection of poems door-to-door while cleaning people's gutters. When he moved from Wigan to Manchester at the age of 21, his poetry was published in a book for the first time.

SAID THE SUN
TO THE MOON

SAID THE HEAD
TO THE HEART

"WE HAVE MORE IN COMMON

THAN SETS US APART"

LEMN SISSAY

MY NAME IS WHY

After that, he wrote many poetry collections, stage plays and a memoir called *My Name is Why* ('Lemn' means 'why' in Amharic, the main language of Ethiopia). He performed his poetry on stages across the world, presenting the first National Poetry Slam in 2004.

Although Lemn found his birth family eventually, the years they had spent apart meant that it was now just too hard for him to form close bonds with them. But for the first time, Lemn began to see that he was loved. People were deeply moved by his poetry and performances. They valued his powerful work, and painted lines from it on many buildings in Manchester. Lemn's poems are also carved into buildings across London, like the Royal Festival Hall, and in other places around the world.

> "I investigated the world through my imagination."

MORE THAN ONE WAY TO LEARN

In 2010, Lemn was awarded an MBE for services to literature, and he was asked to be the first official poet of the 2012 London Olympics. He even wrote the official poem for the 2015 FA Cup! That same year, he was also made Chancellor of the University of Manchester, a hugely important position – and one that amazed Lemn, since he had never been to university himself. But his appointment proved that there is more than one way to learn, and that people who begin life with nothing can make art that speaks to everyone.

Lemn was keen to help other people who had grown up in foster care like him. In 2013, he set up a project called 'The Christmas Dinners for Care Leavers', so that young adult care leavers who may not have families to visit can celebrate together on Christmas Day. For years, Lemn had wanted an apology from the council that had let him down, and in 2018, he finally got it. Wigan Council sent Lemn the files about his early life, gave him money as compensation, and apologised for the ways in which it had failed him as a child. Although no one can give Lemn back his stolen family and childhood, he is now beloved and celebrated, and his work has given hope and joy to thousands.

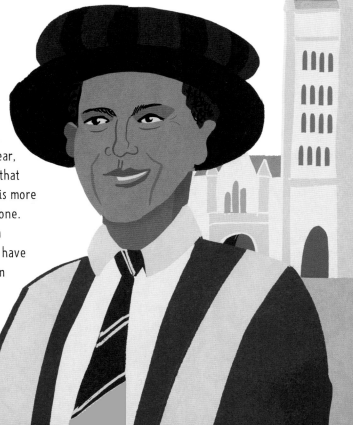

TANNI GREY-THOMPSON

Born with a condition called spina bifida, Tanni Grey-Thompson is an amazingly successful athlete and a powerful campaigner for the rights of people with disabilities. She is also a TV presenter – and a member of the House of Lords!

NEVER HELD BACK

In the summer of 1969, in Cardiff, Wales, a baby girl was born. She was christened Carys Davina, but when her older sister first saw her, she called her "Tiny" instead. "Tiny" turned to "Tanni" – and that was what the baby's name became!

Tanni had been born with spina bifida, which meant that her spine hadn't developed properly. From the age of seven, she needed to use a wheelchair to get around, but Tanni's parents didn't want that to hold her back. They wanted her to try and achieve whatever she wanted to – their attitude was always "get on with it!" They had to fight for a long time for Tanni to attend a mainstream school, rather than a school for children with disabilities, but both Tanni and her parents were determined that it was where she belonged.

When Tanni was 13, she began wheelchair racing. She represented Wales when she was 15 in the Junior National Wheelchair Games and won the 100-metre race – the first of many, many wins for Tanni.

As well as wheelchair racing, Tanni enjoyed other sports as a child, including horse riding, archery, basketball and swimming.

FIRST MEDAL

When she was still a teenager, Tanni had to have an operation in which a steel rod was used to help straighten her spine. After she recovered, she was determined to compete in bigger races, so she joined a sports club in Cardiff for athletes who used wheelchairs. (Sometimes she and her friends raced each other on the ramps in multi-storey car parks – which was very dangerous!) She was soon in training for the 1988 Seoul Paralympics – and she came home from the competition with her first bronze medal.

RACING CAREER

Tanni had to have another operation on her back after that, which stopped her competing for a year. But when she returned, there was no stopping her. In the Barcelona Paralympics in 1992 she took home FOUR gold medals – in the 100 metres, 200 metres, 400 metres and 800 metres!

During her racing career, Tanni won a total of 16 medals, 11 of which were gold medals, at five Paralympic Games between 1988 and 2004. She also won another 12 medals at the World Championships – and won the London Marathon women's wheelchair race six times!

Tanni broke more than 30 world records during her athletic career. She is Britain's greatest ever Paralympic athlete.

"Being in a wheelchair has given me more mobility, not less. It's never stopped me from doing anything I wanted to do."

FIGHTING FOR RIGHTS

In 2007, Tanni announced that she was retiring from sport – but she certainly wasn't disappearing from public life. She presented TV programmes, worked with charities, and campaigned for access to sport for people with disabilities. Her quick wit and determination made her as popular and successful on screen as she had been on the track. In recognition of her achievements, she was made first a Dame, and then a Baroness.

In 2013, Tanni gave a speech in Parliament about the ways in which people with disabilities are still often insulted or poorly treated. She talks openly about hurtful or ignorant things that people have said to her and to other people with disabilities, and fights fiercely for their rights, for women and children's rights, and for the people in society who need help and don't get it.

KELLY HOLMES

Despite setbacks and injuries, the brilliant athlete Kelly Holmes went from driving trucks in the British Army to amazing success on the running track, eventually winning two Olympic gold medals.

SPORTY GIRL

At the start of the 1970s, in a little town called Pembury in Kent, a 17-year-old called Pam had a baby girl. Things were very tough to start with – the baby's father, a mechanic, left before little Kelly was one. Pam's parents suggested she should have Kelly adopted, but Pam loved her daughter and refused to give her up. When Kelly was four, Pam married a painter called Mick Norris, who became Kelly's father – and, after Pam and Mick had two baby boys, their family was complete.

Kelly loved her brothers, treating them like dolls, and they followed her everywhere, wanting to do everything she did. A rough-and-tumble girl, she liked playing with her friends at school, but she didn't work too hard at her lessons – in fact, she was known for mucking about! She was always brilliant at sports, though, and was games captain at her primary school. When she was 12, she joined Tonbridge Athletics Club. Soon, she won the English Schools 1,500-metre race at both junior and senior levels, encouraged by a PE teacher who believed she could succeed in anything. At 14, Kelly wanted to train to be an Olympic champion, but coaching cost a lot of money and Kelly wasn't able to pay for it. So when she was 18, she joined the British Army.

> *Kelly had other jobs as a teenager. She helped nurse people with disabilities – and also worked as an assistant in a sweet shop!*

GO KELLY

TOUGH SERGEANT

At first Kelly was a truck driver, but then became an army fitness instructor. Sergeant Holmes was respected, but known for being tough! After a few years, Kelly decided to return to athletics again, and in 1992 she took up serious training. By 1994, she had won gold in the 1,500 metres at the Commonwealth Games – and was still in the army!

> *As well as winning races, Kelly was great at volleyball and became the army's female judo champion – she was an amazing all-round athlete.*

A FEW SETBACKS

But the next few years were hard for Kelly. Although she set British records for the 800 metres and 1,000 metres in 1995, a fractured bone stopped her winning a medal in the 1996 Atlanta Olympics. Just when she should have been winning international competitions, she had to spend months with her leg in plaster. In 1997, when she finally left the army to devote herself to athletics full-time, she set the UK record for the 1,500 metres – but another serious injury at the Athens World Championships slammed the brakes on again.

However hard she worked to get fitter and stronger, injuries continued to slow Kelly down. Her mental health suffered too – she got very depressed in 2003, just before the World Championships, when she had yet another injury. At the age of 33 – past the peak for many professional athletes – it seemed Kelly's dreams of winning an Olympic gold medal were gone for good.

MAKING HISTORY

But then, at the Athens Olympic Games in 2004, Kelly made history! In an incredibly close race, she won the gold medal in the 800 metres – and, five days later, a second gold in the 1,500 metres! That night, she slept with her medals on her bedside table, unable to believe she had finally realised her childhood dream – and become one of the most successful British track athletes of all time.

Not long afterwards, Kelly was given a damehood by the Queen. Soon after that, she set up the Dame Kelly Holmes Trust, a charity that helps young people facing difficulties in their lives by giving them the chance to be mentored by world-class athletes.

Although she is now retired from professional athletics, Dame Kelly continues to inspire and motivate people – and to run. (But although she is such a brilliant athlete, she hates swimming and really doesn't like getting wet!)

> *Kelly is now an honorary colonel in the Royal Armoured Corps Training Regiment, making her Colonel Dame Kelly Holmes – the only Colonel Dame in the world.*

MO FARAH

Although Mo Farah left Somalia for Britain when he was only a child, and at first found it hard to adapt to his new home, he worked and trained and ran his way to victory, becoming one of the best long-distance runners in the world.

THE TWINS

In 1983, identical twin boys were born to Aisha and Mukhtar Farah in Mogadishu, the capital of Somalia. One brother was called Hassan, the other was called Mohamed – but this soon got shortened to Mo! The twins and their four younger brothers and sisters grew up in the countryside in Somaliland until a war started, and violence tore their home apart. Then Mo and Hassan were sent across the border to the small country of Djibouti, to stay with their grandparents.

Because he was dyslexic, Mo struggled at school, and Hassan had to help him with his reading. He really wanted to be a mechanic, but his family didn't approve of this idea. He was already starting to be good at running, though. When electricity power cuts meant Mo's favourite television show cut out, he'd run to the next street over, then the next, then the next, until he found a street with power – early training for his later victories!

The war in Somalia continued, and, when Mo was eight, he and his two younger brothers were sent overseas to Britain to live with their father, who had been born there. But Hassan was too ill to travel. Mo wouldn't see his beloved twin brother again for 12 whole years.

When he was five or six, Mo was badly burned on his arm in an accident at home. He had a lucky escape, though – if the burn had been a little higher, the nerves in his arm would have been damaged and he might never have been able to run at all.

TIME TO RUN

It took Mo a while to learn English, and he often got into trouble at school because he felt frustrated. He had always loved football, but when he was 11, his PE teacher, Alan Watkinson, suggested he take up running instead. Mr Watkinson drove him to training sessions and encouraged him to work hard. He became such an important figure in Mo's life that when Mo got married in 2010, Mr Watkinson was his best man!

In 1997, Mo won an inter-school cross-country championship. Four years later, when he was 18, he won the European Junior 5,000 metres, with the help of a new coach, Alan Storey. It was clear now that the little boy who'd struggled to fit in had the potential to become a world-class athlete.

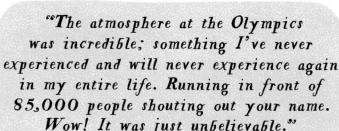

> *"The atmosphere at the Olympics was incredible; something I've never experienced and will never experience again in my entire life. Running in front of 85,000 people shouting out your name. Wow! It was just unbelievable."*

ON THE TRACK TO SUCCESS

Mo continued his training in Kenya and Ethiopia, but he didn't get beyond the semi-finals at his first Olympic Games, in 2008. Determined to do better, he began working with a new coach, and he then won the 5,000-metre race at the World Championships in Daegu, South Korea, in 2011.

Mo was now an incredibly successful runner, at the peak of his fitness. At the London 2012 Olympic Games, with the home crowd cheering wildly for him, he became a double gold medallist, winning both the 5,000-metre and 10,000-metre races.

He went on to repeat his double-gold-winning feat four years later at the 2016 Olympics in Rio de Janeiro, Brazil! After taking gold and silver medals in the 2017 World Championships, Mo switched to running marathons, and won the Chicago Marathon the year after. He was voted BBC Sports Personality of the Year, and was also knighted by the Queen, becoming Sir Mo Farah – and he has won the European Athlete of the Year Trophy three times!

After moving around so much in his early life, and having to say goodbye to homes and family along the way, Mo is now the most successful British track and field athlete of all time. Between 2011 and 2017, he won 10 Olympic and World Championship gold medals!

> *Mo is known for doing the 'Mobot' – making an M with his arms over his head – to celebrate his victories on the track.*

GREAT BRITAIN

FARAH

STORMZY

A famous grime artist and performer, Stormzy fights injustice, racism and inequality wherever he finds them, creating chances for people who need them while he tops the charts with his powerful music.

Apart from Stormzy, Michael has lots of other nicknames, including 'Big Mike', 'The Problem' and 'Wicked Skengman'. 'Big Mike' isn't all that surprising – he's 1.96 metres tall!

NOTHING MORE GANGSTER THAN BEING WELL READ

On a summer day in 1993, a boy called Michael Ebanezer Kwadjo Omari Owuo Jr was born in Croydon, South London. His Ghanaian mum, Abigail, brought him up, taking him to church every week and working three jobs to make sure that Michael, his brother and two sisters always had food to eat. Thornton Heath, their part of Croydon, could be a dangerous place – people often got robbed or hurt – but Michael was happy there, though money was tight at home.

Michael loved school, especially English lessons, where he could write his own poems and stories. He was very competitive and read hundreds of library books to earn prize badges! Although he didn't know it, all that reading was helping develop his gift with words – a gift that would one day make Michael a great rapper and grime artist. As he got older, he was often quite naughty at school, but he still earned several top-grade GCSEs.

One of Michael's favourite authors as a child was Malorie Blackman (page 46). He mentions her in his song "Superheroes".

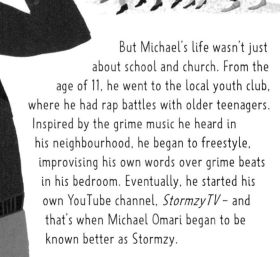

But Michael's life wasn't just about school and church. From the age of 11, he went to the local youth club, where he had rap battles with older teenagers. Inspired by the grime music he heard in his neighbourhood, he began to freestyle, improvising his own words over grime beats in his bedroom. Eventually, he started his own YouTube channel, *StormzyTV* – and that's when Michael Omari began to be known better as Stormzy.

ON THE WAY TO THE TOP

When he was 19, bored and miserable, working at an oil refinery, Stormzy decided it was time to try harder to get his music noticed. Although some people thought grime was rude and rough and the sort of music you couldn't play on the radio, he wanted everyone to hear his songs. So he released a collection of tracks called *168: The Mixtape*, and followed it up the next year with a record, *Dreamers Disease*, which won him a MOBO (Music of Black Origin) Award. Then he was invited to perform on the TV show *Later . . . With Jools Holland*. This was the first time an unsigned artist had ever been on the show! Stormzy was on his way to the top.

When his freestyle single "Shut Up" entered the Top 40 in 2015, Stormzy started a campaign to get it to Christmas Number One. It made it to number eight – incredibly impressive for a freestyle track!

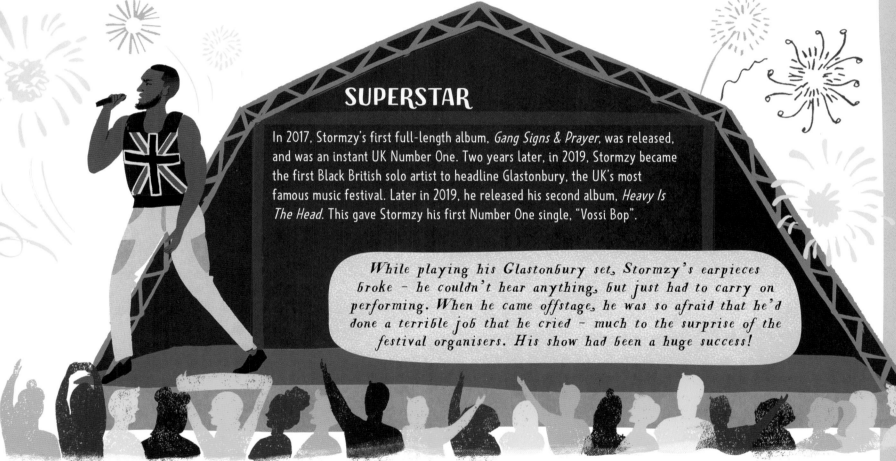

SUPERSTAR

In 2017, Stormzy's first full-length album, *Gang Signs & Prayer*, was released, and was an instant UK Number One. Two years later, in 2019, Stormzy became the first Black British solo artist to headline Glastonbury, the UK's most famous music festival. Later in 2019, he released his second album, *Heavy Is The Head*. This gave Stormzy his first Number One single, "Vossi Bop".

While playing his Glastonbury set, Stormzy's earpieces broke – he couldn't hear anything, but just had to carry on performing. When he came offstage, he was so afraid that he'd done a terrible job that he cried – much to the surprise of the festival organisers. His show had been a huge success!

NEW OPPORTUNITIES

By now, Stormzy had achieved many amazing things, earned a lot of money and brought the love of grime music to people who had never heard it before. Looking back at his childhood, and realising many talented Black children were missing out on their chances to shine, he decided to use his fame and money to do something about it. He set up a scholarship for Black students to study at the University of Cambridge and started #Merky Books with the publisher Penguin Random House, to publish books and poetry by writers whose voices aren't often heard. In 2020, when people around the world protested against racism, Stormzy pledged to donate £10 million to anti-racist charities.

MALALA YOUSAFZAI

Resisting attempts to scare her and keep her quiet, including an attack that nearly killed her, the activist Malala Yousafzai has fought fiercely for every girl's right to an education since she was 11 years old.

DEFYING THE TALIBAN

In July 1997, in the city of Mingora in the beautiful, mountainous Swat District of Pakistan, a baby girl was born, the eldest child of Ziauddin and Toor Pekai Yousafzai. Girls in Pakistan were not always valued as highly as boys, but the baby's father, a poet and teacher, believed passionately in education for everyone. He wanted to give his daughter exactly the same opportunities that he would later give his sons.

Young Malala loved school and was a gifted, hard-working student. She shared her father's passion for education, and his belief that it was for everyone.

Ten years after Malala was born, an extremist political group called the Taliban took control of the Swat District. The Taliban believed that girls should not be educated, and that everyone should obey strict religious rules about how they dress and behave. They banned TV, music, make-up, and even flying kites, and harshly punished people who disobeyed. They also began stopping girls from going to school. In 2008, Malala started speaking out against the invaders who had taken away her right to be educated. As the Taliban closed school after school, she wrote down her sad, fearful, angry thoughts, and shared them on a BBC blog. Speaking out in this way was dangerous, but Malala felt that she should tell the world what the Taliban was taking away from the girls of the Swat Valley.

In October 2012, the Taliban tried to silence Malala forever. When she was on her way home from school, an armed man got onto her bus, terrifying the girls, and asked them: "Who is Malala?" He shot her in the head with his gun – but Malala did not die. Ten days later, she woke up in a hospital in Birmingham, UK. Her injuries were very serious, and doctors and nurses had worked desperately to save her life. Offers to help the brave 15-year-old activist had come from hospitals around the world. Malala took a long time to recover, but when she was better, she and her family made a new home in Britain.

THE MALALA FUND

Although Malala considered the UK her second home, she missed the beauty of her mountain valley, and the tastes and smells of the home she had been forced to leave. But she was also determined to seize the chances her new home offered, and to continue fighting for what she believed in. She and her father set up an organisation called the Malala Fund, dedicated to making sure every girl has access to 12 years of free and safe education. The organisation concentrates on the countries where girls are most likely to miss out on going to school as they get older. As well as meeting and helping the girls themselves, they support and train teachers and activists in these places to help their students too. Malala wants to ensure that every girl in the world can choose the future she wants – and have the right education for it.

NOBEL PEACE PRIZE

In 2013, on her 16th birthday, Malala made a speech to the United Nations, in which she called on the world's leaders to put aside their disagreements, to fight for education and to make sure that women's rights are protected. She also presented a petition to the UN Secretary-General demanding education for all. It had more than 3 million signatures! The day was called 'Malala Day' in her honour.

At age 17, she was given the Nobel Peace Prize – the youngest person ever to receive it. She went on to study at Oxford University, while at the same time continuing to fight injustice for women and girls across the world. In 2020, Malala graduated from university, completing her own education, and one of her hopes for the future is that every other girl should be able to do the same.

Malala is also a published author! Her books include *I Am Malala*, the story of her life, and *We Are Displaced*, which tells the stories of many women throughout the world who have had to leave their homes.

GLOSSARY

activist A person who campaigns publicly or works for an organisation to bring about social or political change.

adoption The act of taking another person's child into your family and him or her legally becoming your own child.

artificial intelligence A type of technology that makes computers work in a way similar to how human minds work, including making decisions, translating languages and recognising speech.

boarding school A school where pupils live in – sleeping and eating all meals there – during the school term.

cabinet A group of the most senior, or important, ministers in a government who meet to decide its policies.

CERN European Organization for Nuclear Research (the initials stand for French Conseil Européen pour la Recherche Nucléaire), an organisation of European states which does research into high-energy particle physics, based at a centre in Geneva, Switzerland.

civil war A war between different groups of people living in the same country.

conservation An effort to protect and preserve something that is valuable, especially the natural environment.

COVID-19 An infectious disease discovered in 2019, caused by a virus called a coronavirus. In 2020, the disease spread quickly to almost every country in the world, which is called a pandemic.

Dame A title given to a woman in recognition of important work she has done or for service to her country.

depression A mental state in which the sufferer feels very sad and unable to enjoy life.

documentary A television or radio programme or a film that gives factual information about a particular subject.

dyslexic A dyslexic person has a learning difference called dyslexia, which affects reading and writing skills.

empire A number of individual nations that are controlled by the government or ruler of a single country.

entrepreneur A person who starts a business.

feminist A person who believes that men and women are equal and that women should therefore have the same power, rights and opportunities as men.

First World War (1914–1918) The war fought between the Central Powers (led by Germany) and the Allied Powers (led by Great Britain, France, Russia and the USA) over control of Europe, with the Allied Powers winning. Over 16 million people died.

foster family When a child lives with a foster family, he or she becomes part of the family for a period of time without legally becoming the child of their foster parents.

grime A type of music that combines elements of garage, hip-hop, rap and jungle.

immigrant A person who comes from one country to live in another.

independence People who seek independence for their country wish to have their own government and not be ruled by another country.

knight A man may be made a knight in recognition of important work he has done or for service to his country, and he can then use the title Sir.

LGBT+ Lesbian, gay, bisexual, transgender plus any other sexual and gender identities.

Nazi A member of the National Socialist German Workers' Party, a harsh and aggressive political movement led by the dictator Adolf Hitler, which controlled Germany from 1933 to 1945.

Nobel Prize One of six awards given each year to people who have done important work in science, literature, economics, or for world peace.

Olympic Games An important international sports festival held every four years, each time in a different country. Events include athletics, football, swimming and gymnastics.

Paralympic Games An important international sports festival for athletes with disabilities, held every four years with the Olympic Games.

parliament The group of people who make decisions for a country and make or change its laws; the building in which these people meet and work.

petition A document signed by lots of people to ask a government or other organisation to do, or not do, a particular thing.

physics The scientific study of forces such as light, sound, heat, pressure, gravity and electricity and the way in which they affect objects.

programming The process of writing a computer program – a series of coded instructions needed for a computer to perform a task.

racism Prejudice or discrimination against someone of a different skin colour or physical appearance; the belief that one's own race is superior to another.

refugee Someone who has been forced to leave their home or country to escape a natural disaster, war or persecution.

rights Things that every member of society is morally allowed to have, such as freedom and equality.

Second World War (1939–1945) The war fought between the Axis Powers (Germany, Italy and Japan) and the Allied Powers (France, Great Britain, the USA and Russia), partly in continuation of the problems of the First World War. The Allies eventually won the war. Around 50 million people were killed.

social worker A person whose job is to give help and advice to people who are suffering from serious family or financial problems.

software Computer programs and operating information.

statistics The practice or science of collecting and analysing large numbers of facts and figures.

trade union An organisation of workers in a trade or profession formed to protect their rights and to represent them in discussions with their employers, often to improve wages and working conditions.

vaccine A type of medicine that is usually injected into a person's body while they are healthy, and teaches a person's body how to fight off a particular virus that could cause a disease.

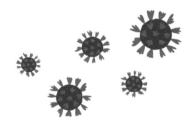

virus Tiny particles that can cause disease in people, animals and plants.

World Wide Web A computer system on the internet that links documents and pictures into a database that people all over the world can use.

Zoroastrianism A religion founded in Persia by the prophet Zoroaster in the 6th century BCE. Zoroastrians believe in one god, called Ahura Mazda, and are guided by the principle: good thoughts, good words, good deeds.

INDEX